Crochet Snowflakes
Step-by-Step

Crochet Snowflakes
Step-by-Step

A delightful flurry of 40 patterns

**Waterford City and County
Libraries**

Caitlin Sainio

Search Press

Contents

Crochet Snowflakes Step-by-Step

A QUARTO BOOK

First published in 2016 by
Search Press Ltd
Wellwood
North Farm Road
Kent TN2 3DR

Copyright © 2016
Quarto Publishing plc

ISBN 978-1-78221-437-3

10 9 8 7 6 5 4 3 2 1

Conceived, designed
and produced by
Quarto Publishing plc
The Old Brewery
6 Blundell Street
London N7 9BH

www.quartoknows.com

QUAR.SBSS

Senior Project Editor:
Chelsea Edwards
Senior Art Editor: Emma Clayton
Designer: Julie Francis
Photographers: Phil Wilkins,
Simon Pask
Illustrator: Kuo Kang Chen
Design Assistant: Martina Calvio
Pattern Checker: Leonie Morgan
Copyeditor: Claire Waite Brown
Proofreader: Caroline West
Indexer: Helen Snaith

Art Director: Caroline Guest
Creative Director: Moira Clinch
Publisher: Paul Carslake

Colour separation in Singapore
by Pica Digital Pte Limited

Printed in China by Toppan
Leefung Printing Limited

Page **18**

Beginner patterns

18 Chamonix

28 St Paul

30 Minneapolis

40 Windwhistle

42 Muuk

50 Ben Lomond

52 Altay

20 Reykjavik

22 Sapporo

24 Banff

26 Bariloche

32 Tallinn

34 Sokcho

36 Winnipeg

38 St Petersburg

Page 44

Intermediate patterns

44 Karaj

46 Munich

48 Portillo

54 Montreal

56 Innsbruck

58 Nome

60 Harbin

6

62 Chrea

64 El Serrat

66 Aspen

68 Uppsala

72 Charlotte Pass

74 St John's

76 Irkutsk

78 Capracotta

84 Caribou

86 Erzurum

88 Kiev

90 Helsinki

Page **70**

Advanced patterns

70 Dingboche

80 Prague

82 Bamiyan

92 Syracuse

94 Hammerfest

97 San Martin

Caitlin's crochet world

I learned to crochet as a child, first from elementary school classmates, and later from craft books. As someone who loved art, mathematics and textiles, I found crochet to be a captivating combination of the three. I was fascinated by the beautiful designs that crocheters could create, just by making a series of knots. I was even more excited to discover that the process was mathematical: that different stitches took up different amounts of space, and that they could be joined to create predictable shapes. Best of all, crocheting gave me an excuse to collect beautiful threads and yarns, which I could transform, stitch by stitch, into soft, textured lace.

My earliest thread crochet projects were snowflake ornaments, many of which still hang on my parents' Christmas tree each year. I come from an area famous for its long, snowy winters, and I associate crochet snowflakes with the warmest parts of those winters: Christmas decorating, holiday gift giving and winter evenings spent crocheting near a warm stove.

I hope the snowflakes in this collection will bring the same warmth and brightness to your winters, and that you enjoy making them as much as I've enjoyed designing them.

Caitlin Sainio

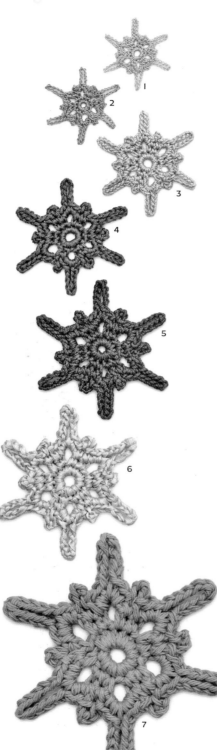

Tools and materials

One of the attractions of crochet snowflakes is that they do not require a large collection of specialised tools or materials. Select a steel hook and a ball of crochet thread, gather a few common household supplies and you will be ready to begin.

Crochet thread (A)

Snowflakes are usually crocheted from cotton crochet thread, which comes in sizes from 3 to 100, with higher numbers indicating finer threads. Thicker threads are easiest to crochet and, for that reason, all of the patterns in this collection were designed for size 10 thread. Experiment with finer threads and smaller hooks to create smaller, lighter-weight snowflakes. Or you may also wish to try other thicker materials, such as yarns, to create a larger snowflake.

Scissors

A small, sharp-pointed pair of scissors is especially helpful for clipping thread ends.

Crochet hooks (B)

For crocheting in thread, you will need a small, steel crochet hook. The patterns in this book use a 1.75mm crochet hook with size 10 thread. Thread thicknesses vary, as do the tensions of individual crocheters, so any hook size recommendation should be taken as a starting point only. For the purposes of these snowflakes, the correct hook is the one that allows you to work most comfortably with your chosen thread.

Starch or fabric stiffener

In order to hold their shapes, most snowflakes need to be stiffened. The material you use as a stiffener will depend on how you plan to use the snowflake, and on your personal preference. Laundry starch (either liquid starch or heavy spray starch) can be used to stiffen snowflakes for hanging or for use as appliqués, while preserving the thread's soft feel. Homemade sugar starches (recipes are available online) produce a similar effect. Commercial fabric stiffeners will give the snowflakes a hard or semi-hard finish, which can be useful for jewellery, hair accessories or hanging applications. (A mixture of white glue and water can be used as a substitute for fabric stiffener.)

Straight pins (C)

Use straight pins made from stainless steel, nickel-plated brass or another rust-proof material to hold your snowflake in position during blocking. It is a good idea to test the pins before use, to ensure that they will not stain the snowflakes. To do this, pin some to a piece of white fabric or a crochet sample, dampen it with your choice of stiffener, let it dry and then check for rust spots or stains.

Blocking board components

Snowflakes are best blocked on a blocking board, which can be made quickly and cheaply using readily available materials. You will need paper, tape, corrugated cardboard or cork board, cling film and the instructions on page 15.

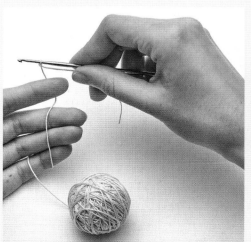

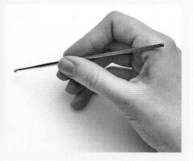

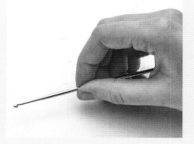

Core techniques

For readers who are new to crochet (and those who could use a review), this section provides instruction on the stitches used in this book, as well as information about blocking and finishing. If you have never crocheted before, start by working the stitches with a large crochet hook in medium-weight yarn. Once you are comfortable with them, switch to thread.

Holding the hook and yarn

Holding the hook as if it were a pen is the most widely used method. Centre the tips of your right thumb and forefinger over the flat section of the hook.

An alternative way to hold the hook is to grasp the flat section of the hook between your right thumb and forefinger as if you were holding a knife.

Thread and hook sizes used for snowflake samples opposite: I size 40 crochet cotton; 1.25mm hook 2 size 30 crochet cotton; 1.25mm hook 3 size 10 crochet cotton; 1.75mm hook 4 cotton embroidery thread; 1.75mm hook 5 size 3 crochet cotton; 2mm hook 6 3mm ('/₈in) polyester ribbon; 2mm hook 7 medium-weight cotton yarn; 4mm hook

To control the supply and keep an even tension on the yarn, loop the short end of the yarn over your left forefinger and take the yarn coming from the ball loosely around the little finger on the same hand. Use the middle finger on the same hand to help hold the work. If left-handed, hold the hook in the left hand and the yarn in the right.

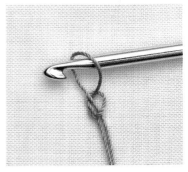

Making a slip knot

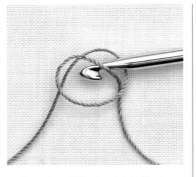

1 Loop the yarn as shown.

2 Insert the hook into the loop, catch the yarn with the hook and pull it through to make a loop over the hook.

3 Gently pull the yarn to tighten the loop around the hook and complete the slip knot.

Working a foundation chain (ch)

The foundation chain is the equivalent of casting on in knitting, and it is important to make sure that you have made the required number of chains for the pattern you are going to work. Count each V-shaped loop on the front of the chain as one chain stitch, except for the loop on the hook, which is not counted. You may find it easier to turn the chain over and count the stitches on the back of the chain – each raised 'bump' on the back of the chain counts as one stitch. When working the first row of stitches (usually called the foundation row) into the chain, insert the hook under one thread or two, depending on your preference.

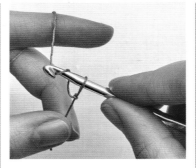

1 Holding the hook with the slip knot in your right hand and the yarn in your left, wrap the yarn over the hook. Draw the yarn through the loop on the hook to make a new loop and complete the first chain stitch.

2 Continue in this way, drawing a new loop of yarn through the loop on the hook until the chain is the required length. Move the thumb and second finger that are grasping the chain upwards after every few stitches to keep the tension even. When working into the chain, insert the hook under one thread (for a looser edge) or two (for a firmer edge), depending on your preference.

Working a slip stitch (sl st)

Slip stitch is the shortest of all the crochet stitches and its main uses are for joining rounds, making seams and carrying the hook and yarn from one place to another.

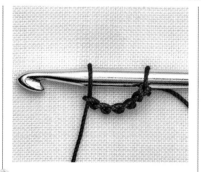

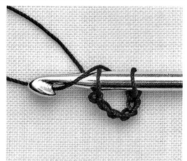

1 Insert the hook from front to back into the required stitch.

2 Wrap the yarn over the hook (yarn over) and draw it through both the work and the loop on the hook. One loop remains on the hook and one slip stitch has been worked.

Working a double crochet (dc)

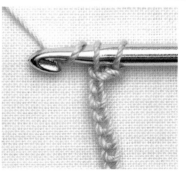

1 Begin with a foundation chain (see page 10) and insert the hook from front to back into the second chain from the hook. Wrap the yarn over the hook (yarn over) and draw it through the first loop, leaving two loops on the hook.

2 To complete the stitch, yarn over and draw it through both loops on the hook, leaving one loop on the hook. Continue in this way, working one double crochet into each chain.

3 At the end of the row, turn and work one chain for the turning chain (note that this chain does not count as a stitch). Insert the hook into the first double crochet at the beginning of the row. Work a double crochet into each stitch of the previous row, being careful to work the final stitch into the last stitch of the row, not into the turning chain.

Working a half treble crochet (htr)

 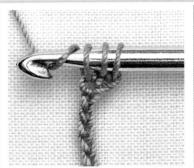 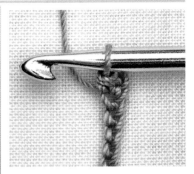

1 Begin with a foundation chain (see page 10), wrap the yarn over the hook (yarn over) and insert the hook into the third chain from the hook.

2 Draw the yarn through the chain, leaving three loops on the hook. Yarn over and draw through all three loops on the hook, leaving one loop on the hook. One half treble stitch complete. Continue along the row, working one half treble crochet into each chain.

3 At the end of the row, work two chains to turn. Skip the first stitch and work a half treble crochet into each stitch made on the previous row. At the end of the row, work the last stitch into the top of the turning chain.

Working a treble crochet (tr)

1 Begin with a foundation chain (see page 10), wrap the yarn over the hook and insert the hook into the fourth chain from the hook.

2 Draw the yarn through the chain, leaving three loops on the hook. Yarn over again and draw the yarn through the first two loops on the hook, leaving two loops on the hook.

3 Yarn over and draw the yarn through the two loops on the hook, leaving one loop on the hook. One treble crochet complete. Continue along the row, working one treble crochet stitch into each chain. At the end of the row, work three chains to turn. Skip the first stitch and work a treble crochet into each stitch made on the previous row. At the end of the row, work the last stitch into the top of the turning chain.

Working a double treble crochet (dtr)

1 Begin with a foundation chain (see page 10), wrap the yarn over the hook twice (yarn over twice) and insert the hook into the fifth chain from the hook.

2 Draw the yarn through the chain, leaving four loops on the hook. Yarn over again and draw the yarn through the first two loops on the hook, leaving three loops on the hook.

3 Yarn over again and draw through the first two loops on the hook, leaving two loops on the hook.

4 Yarn over again and draw through the two remaining loops, leaving one loop on the hook. Double treble crochet is now complete.

5 Continue along the row, working one double treble crochet stitch into each chain. At the end of the row, work four chains to turn. Skip the first stitch and work a double treble into each stitch made on the previous row. At the end of the row, work the last stitch into the top of the turning chain.

Working in rounds

Snowflakes are worked in rounds, which means that they are worked outwards from a central ring called a foundation ring.

Making a foundation ring
Work a short length of foundation chain (see page 10) as specified in the pattern. Join the chains into a ring by working a slip stitch into the first stitch of the foundation chain.

1 **Working into the ring**
Work the number of turning chains specified in the pattern – three chains are shown here (counting as a treble crochet stitch). Inserting the hook into the space at the centre of the ring each time, work the number of stitches specified in the pattern into the ring.

2 Count the stitches at the end of the round to check you have worked the correct number. Join the first and last stitches of the round together by working a slip stitch into the top of the turning chain.

Finishing off the final round
To make a neat edge, finish off the final round by using this method of sewing the first and last stitches together in preference to the slip stitch joining method shown above.

1 Cut the yarn, leaving an end of about 10cm (4in), and draw it through the last stitch. With right side facing, thread the end in a tapestry needle and take it under both loops of the stitch next to the turning chain.

2 Pull the needle through and insert it into the centre of the last stitch of the round. On the wrong side, pull the needle through to complete the stitch, adjust the length of the stitch to close the round and then weave in the end on the wrong side in the usual way.

Blocking and stiffening

To make your snowflake flat, neat and symmetrical (and to ensure that it stays that way during hanging), it is necessary to block and stiffen it.

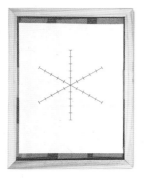

1 Make a blocking board. Copy the blocking diagram shown here on to a sheet of paper. Tape the paper to a flat piece of corrugated cardboard, cork board or any other rigid, pin-friendly material, such as polystyrene.

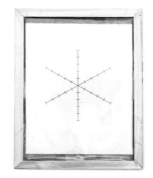

2 Cover it with cling film, so that it will be waterproof.

3 Soak the snowflake with strong laundry starch solution, fabric stiffener or (for applications that do not require a stiff snowflake) water.

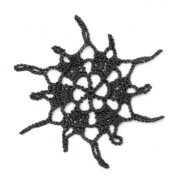

4 Gently squeeze out any excess liquid, and press the snowflake approximately to shape.

5 Lay the snowflake on the blocking board, on the centre of the blocking diagram. Use the diagram's lines as guides to aid in symmetrical placement of the snowflake's arms.

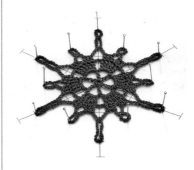

6 Adjust the snowflake until it is flat and even, with straight arms and neat loops. Secure the snowflake to the board with straight pins. Let it dry completely before removing it.

1
Snowflake patterns

The snowflakes in this chapter are organised by level of difficulty. Leaf through and choose your favourite designs, or start with the basic patterns and work your way up to the advanced ones, learning new techniques as you go.

1 Chamonix

Skill level: ❄

This simple snowflake is composed of the three most basic stitches: the chain, the slip stitch and the double crochet. The pattern is designed for size 10 crochet thread, but if you are new to crochet, you may find it easier to make it with yarn first.

Materials:
- Thread required: 3.7m (4yd)

Tools:
- 1.75mm crochet hook

Finished diameter: 57mm (2¼in)

Foundation ring: ch 10, and join with sl st in first ch. (See Steps 1–2.)

Rnd 1: ch 1 (counts as dc). [ch 12, dc] 5 times in ring. ch 12 and join with sl st in initial ch 1. (See Steps 3–4.)

Rnd 2: ch 1 (counts as dc). *ch 7. [dc, ch 10, dc] in top of next ch-12 point. ch 7.** dc in next dc. Repeat from * 4 more times, and from * to ** once. Join with sl st in initial ch 1. Fasten off; weave in ends. (See Steps 4–8.)

Chart key:

- ⌒ **ch** Chain
- • **sl st** Slip stitch
- + **dc** Double crochet

1 ch 10.

2 sl st in the first chain of the ch 10, to form the foundation ring.

3 ch 1 (this counts as the first dc of Rnd 1). [ch 12, dc] in the foundation ring, five times. Then ch 12.

4 sl st in the ch 1 that began the round. ch 1 (this counts as the first dc of Rnd 2).

5 *ch 7. Work [dc, ch 10, dc] in the top of the next ch-12 point.

6 ch 7.** dc in the next dc.

7 Repeat Steps 5 and 6 four more times.

8 Begin a fifth repeat of Steps 5 and 6, but stop before making the final dc of Step 6. sl st in the ch 1 that began the round. Fasten off and weave in ends.

2 Reykjavik

Skill level: ❋

This little crystal features a compact central star with points made from long, chained loops. This pattern provides an opportunity for you to practise with asterisks, which are often used in crochet patterns to indicate repeats and partial repeats.

Materials:
- Thread required: 2.7m (3yd)

Tools:
- 1.75mm crochet hook

Finished diameter: 48mm (1⅞in)

Foundation ring: ch 6, and join with sl st in first ch. (See Step I.)

Rnd I: ch I (counts as dc). II dc in ring. Join with sl st in initial ch I. (See Step 2.)

Rnd 2: ch I (counts as dc). dc in I dc. *ch 4, and dc in 2 dc. Repeat from * 4 more times. ch 4, and join with sl st in initial ch I. (See Steps 3–5.)

Rnd 3: ch I (counts as dc). *ch 4. dc in next dc. [2 dc, ch 10, 2 dc] in ch-4 point.** dc in I dc. Repeat from * 4 more times, and from * to ** once. Join with sl st in initial ch I. Fasten off; weave in ends. (See Steps 6–8.)

Chart key:
- ⌒ **ch** Chain
- • **sl st** Slip stitch
- + **dc** Double crochet

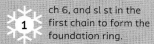

1 ch 6, and sl st in the first chain to form the foundation ring.

2 ch I (this counts as the first dc of Rnd I). II dc in foundation ring. sl st in the ch I that began the round.

3 ch I (this counts as the first dc of Rnd 2). dc in I dc. *ch 4. dc in 2 dc.

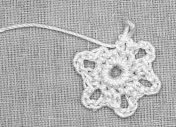

4 Returning to Step 3, repeat all the instructions that come after the * four more times. (You will have a total of five ch-4 points.)

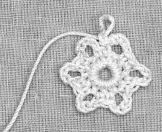

5 ch 4, and sl st in the ch I that began the round, to create the sixth point. ch I (this counts as the first dc of Rnd 3).

6 *ch 4, and dc in the next dc.

7 [2 dc, ch I0, 2 dc] in the next ch-4 point.** dc in the next dc.

8 Repeat Steps 6 and 7 four more times. Begin a fifth repeat, but stop when you get to the ** in Step 7. sl st in the ch I that began the round. Fasten off and weave in ends.

3 Sapporo

Skill level: ❋

In Sapporo, treble crochets and long chains work together to form a clean, rounded design.

Materials:
- Thread required: 6.4m (7yd)

Tools:
- 1.75mm crochet hook

Finished diameter: 70mm (2¾in)

Foundation ring: ch 6, and join with sl st in first ch. (See Step 1.)

Rnd 1: ch 3 (counts as tr). tr in ring. [ch 3, 2 tr] 5 times in ring. ch 3. Join with sl st in top of initial ch 3. (See Steps 1–2.)

Rnd 2: ch 3 (counts as tr). tr in next tr. *[2 tr, ch 9, 2 tr] in ch-3 point.** tr in 2 tr. Repeat from * 4 more times, and from * to ** once. Join with sl st in top of initial ch 3. (See Steps 3–5.)

Rnd 3: sl st in 1 tr. *ch 4. Skip 2 tr. [3 tr, ch 6, 3 tr] in next ch-9 loop. ch 4. Skip 2 tr.** sl st in 2 tr. Repeat from * 4 more times, and from * to ** once. Join with sl st in sl st. Fasten off; weave in ends. (See Steps 5–8.)

Chart key:

- ◠ **ch** Chain
- • **sl st** Slip stitch
- ⊤ **tr** Treble crochet

1 ch 6, and sl st in the first chain to form the foundation ring. ch 3 (this counts as the first tr of Rnd I). tr in ring.

2 [ch 3, 2 tr] five times in ring. Then ch 3, and sl st in the third ch of the ch 3 that began the round.

3 ch 3 (this counts as the first tr of Rnd 2). tr in the next tr.

  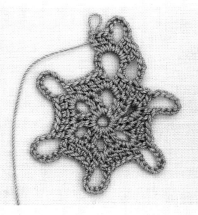

4 *[2 tr, ch 9, 2 tr] in ch-3 point.** tr in 2 tr.

5 Repeat Step 4 four more times. Begin a fifth repeat, but stop when you get to the **. sl st in the top of the ch 3 that began the round, and in the next tr.

6 *ch 4. Skip 2 tr. [3 tr, ch 6, 3 tr] in the next ch-9 loop.

 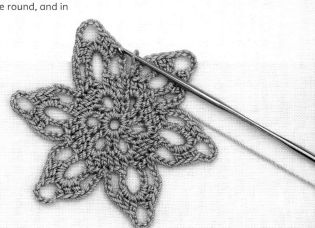

7 ch 4, and skip 2 tr.** sl st in 2 tr.

8 Repeat Steps 6 and 7 four more times. Begin a fifth repeat, but stop when you get to the ** in Step 7. sl st in sl st. Fasten off and weave in ends.

4 Banff

Skill level: ❄

This pattern creates points with picots, which are small loops of chain closed with slip stitches.

Materials:
- Thread required: 4.6m (5yd)

Tools:
- 1.75mm crochet hook

Finished diameter: 70mm (2¾in)

Foundation ring: ch 6, and join with sl st in first ch. (See Step I.)

Rnd I: ch I (counts as dc). II dc in ring. Join with sl st in initial ch I. (See Step I.)

Rnd 2: ch I (counts as dc). dc in I dc. *ch 6. dc in 2 dc. Repeat from * 4 more times. ch 6, and join with sl st in initial ch I. (See Steps 2–4.)

Rnd 3: sl st in I dc and in ch-6 space. ch I (counts as dc). 3 dc in same ch-6 space. *ch II. sl st in 4th ch from hook to form picot. ch 7. 4 dc in same ch-6 space as last dc. ch 8.** 4 dc in next ch-6 space. Repeat from * 4 more times, and from * to ** once. Join with sl st in initial dc. Fasten off; weave in ends. (See Steps 5–8.)

Chart key:

- ◯ **ch** Chain
- • **sl st** Slip stitch
- + **dc** Double crochet

1 ch 6, and sl st in the first chain to form the foundation ring. ch 1 (this counts as the first dc of Rnd 1). 11 dc in foundation ring. sl st in the ch 1 that began the round.

2 ch 1 (this counts as the first dc of Rnd 2). dc in 1 dc.

3 *ch 6. dc in 2 dc.

4 Repeat Step 3 four more times. Then ch 6, and sl st in the ch 1 that began the round.

5 sl st in 1 dc, and in ch-6 space. ch 1 (this counts as the first dc of Rnd 3). 3 dc in same ch-6 space.

6 *ch 11. sl st in fourth ch from hook to form picot. ch 7.

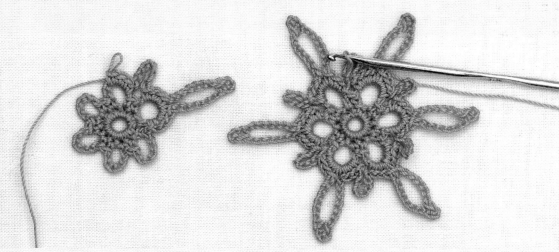

7 4 dc in same ch-6 space as last dc. ch 8.** 4 dc in next ch-6 space.

8 Repeat Steps 6 and 7 four more times. Begin a fifth repeat, but stop when you get to the ** in Step 7. sl st in the ch 1 that began the round. Fasten off and weave in ends.

Bariloche

Skill level: ※

The gentle curves of this star are created from a mix of stitches, including double, treble and double treble crochets.

Materials:
■ Thread required: 6.4m (7yd)

Tools:
■ 1.75mm crochet hook

Finished diameter: 64mm (2½in)

Foundation ring: ch 6, and join with sl st in first ch. (See Step I.)

Rnd I: ch I (counts as dc). II dc in ring. Join with sl st in initial ch I. (See Step I.)

Rnd 2: ch 4 (counts as dtr). [ch 2, dtr] in each of II dc. ch 2, and join with sl st in top of initial ch 4. (See Steps 2–3.)

Rnd 3: ch I (counts as dc). *ch 5. 2 dtr in next dtr. ch 5.** dc in next dtr. Repeat from * 4 more times, and from * to ** once. Join with sl st in initial ch I. (See Steps 3–5.)

Rnd 4: *5 dc in ch-5 space. [dc, tr] in I dtr. ch 3. [tr, dc] in I dtr. 5 dc in ch-5 space.** sl st in dc. Repeat from * 4 more times, and from * to ** once. Join with sl st in sl st. Fasten off; weave in ends. (See Steps 6–8.)

Chart key:

○ **ch** Chain

· **sl st** Slip stitch

+ **dc** Double crochet

tr Treble crochet

dtr Double treble crochet ,

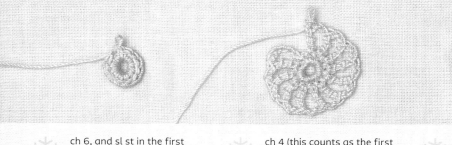

1	ch 6, and sl st in the first chain to form the foundation ring. ch I (this counts as the first dc of Rnd I). II dc in foundation ring. sl st in the ch I that began the round.
2	ch 4 (this counts as the first dtr of Rnd 2). [ch 2, dtr] in each of the II dc.
3	ch 2, and sl st in top of the ch 4 that began the round. ch I (this counts as the first dc of Rnd 3).

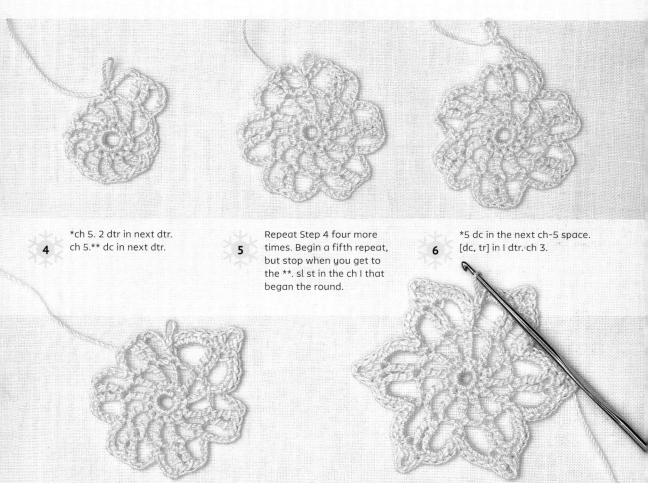

4	*ch 5. 2 dtr in next dtr. ch 5.** dc in next dtr.
5	Repeat Step 4 four more times. Begin a fifth repeat, but stop when you get to the **. sl st in the ch I that began the round.
6	*5 dc in the next ch-5 space. [dc, tr] in I dtr. ch 3.
7	[tr, dc] in the next dtr, and 5 dc in the next ch-5 space.** sl st in dc.
8	Repeat Steps 6 and 7 four more times. Begin a fifth repeat, but stop when you get to the ** in Step 7. sl st in the next sl st. Fasten off and weave in ends.

6 St Paul

Skill level: ❄

Named for the smaller of the Twin Cities of Minneapolis and St Paul, this snowflake features a hexagonal base, decorated with loops of chain.

Materials:
- Thread required: 4.6m (5yd)

Tools:
- 1.75mm crochet hook

Finished diameter: 67mm (2⅝in)

Foundation ring: ch 6, and join with sl st in first ch. (See Step I.)

Rnd I: ch 4 (counts as dtr). dtr in ring. [ch 5, 2 dtr] 5 times in ring. ch 5, and join with sl st in top of initial ch 4. (See Steps I–2.)

Rnd 2: sl st in dtr, and in ch-5 space. ch 3 (counts as tr), and 5 tr in same space. *ch I. 6 tr in next ch-5 space. Repeat from * 4 more times. ch I, and join with sl st in top of initial ch 3. (See Steps 3–5.)

Rnd 3: sl st in 2 tr. *ch I0, and sl st in I0th ch from hook to form picot. sl st in next tr. ch 5. Skip 2 tr, and sl st in ch-I space. ch 5.** Skip 2 tr, and sl st in I tr. Repeat from * 4 more times, and from * to ** once. Skip 2 sl st, and join with sl st in sl st. Fasten off; weave in ends. (See Steps 5–8.)

Chart key:

- ⚬ **ch** Chain
- • **sl st** Slip stitch
- ⊺ **tr** Treble crochet
- ⊺ **dtr** Double treble crochet

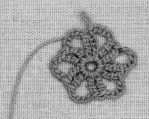
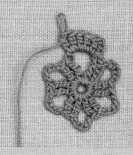

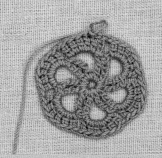

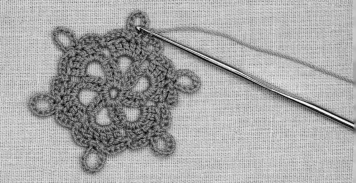

1 ch 6, and sl st in the first chain to form the foundation ring. ch 4 (this counts as the first dtr of Rnd 1). dtr in ring.

2 [ch 5, 2 dtr] five times in ring. ch 5, and sl st in the top of the ch 4 that began the round.

3 sl st in dtr, and in ch-5 space. ch 3 (this counts as the first tr of Rnd 2), and 5 tr in same space.

4 *ch 1. 6 tr in next ch-5 space.

5 Repeat Step 4 four more times. ch 1, sl st in the top of the ch 3 that began the round, and in 2 tr.

6 *ch 10, and sl st in the tenth ch from the hook to form picot.

7 sl st in next tr. ch 5, skip 2 tr, and sl st in ch-1 space. ch 5.** Skip 2 tr, and sl st in 1 tr.

8 Repeat Steps 6 and 7 four more times. Begin a fifth repeat, but stop when you get to the ** in Step 7. Skip 2 sl st, and sl st in 1 sl st. Fasten off and weave in ends.

7 Minneapolis

Skill level: ※

Minneapolis shares its two inner rows with St Paul, but an extra row of stitches and variations in the border make it a design all its own.

Materials:
- Thread required: 8.2m (9yd)

Tools:
- 1.75mm crochet hook

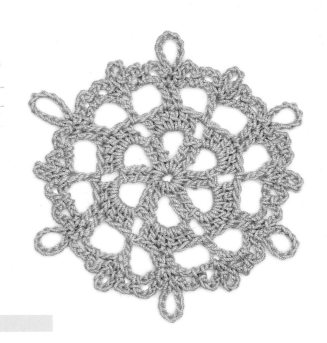

Finished diameter: 83mm (3¼in)

Foundation ring: ch 6, and join with sl st in first ch. (See Step 1.)

Rnd 1: ch 4 (counts as dtr). dtr in ring. [ch 5, 2 dtr] 5 times in ring. ch 5, and join with sl st in top of initial ch 4. (See Step 1.)

Rnd 2: sl st in dtr, and in ch-5 space. ch 3 (counts as tr), and 5 tr in same space. *ch 1. 6 tr in next ch-5 space. Repeat from * 4 more times. ch 1, and join with sl st in top of initial ch 3. (See Step 1.)

Rnd 3: sl st in 2 tr. ch 3 (counts as tr). tr in 1 tr. *ch 6. Skip 2 tr, and tr in ch-1 space. ch 6.** Skip 2 tr, and tr in 2 tr. Repeat from * 4 more times, and from * to ** once. Join with sl st in top of initial ch 3. (See Steps 1–4.)

Rnd 4: ch 1 (counts as dc). *ch 10, and sl st in 10th ch from hook to form picot. dc in next tr. [ch 4, dc, ch 4] in next ch-6 space. [dc, ch 6, dc] in next tr. [ch 4, dc, ch 4] in next ch-6 space.** dc in next tr. Repeat from * 4 more times, and from * to ** once. Join with sl st in initial ch 1. Fasten off; weave in ends. (See Steps 4–8.)

Chart key:
- ○ **ch** Chain
- • **sl st** Slip stitch
- + **dc** Double crochet
- ⊤ **tr** Treble crochet
- ∤ **dtr** Double treble crochet

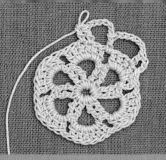

1 Follow Steps 1–5 of St Paul (see page 29).

2 ch 3 (this counts as the first tr of Rnd 3). tr in 1 tr.

3 *ch 6. Skip 2 tr, and tr in ch-1 space. ch 6.** Skip 2 tr, and tr in 2 tr.

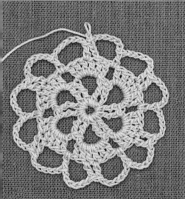

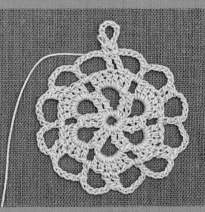

4 Repeat Step 3 four more times. Begin a fifth repeat, but stop when you get to the **. sl st in the top of the ch 3 that began the round. ch 1 (this counts as the first dc of Rnd 4).

5 *ch 10, and sl st in the tenth ch from hook to form picot. dc in next tr.

6 [ch 4, dc, ch 4] in next ch-6 space. [dc, ch 6, dc] in next tr.

7 [ch 4, dc, ch 4] in next ch-6 space.** dc in next tr.

8 Repeat Steps 5–7 four more times. Begin a fifth repeat, but stop when you get to the ** in Step 7. sl st in the ch 1 that began the round. Fasten off and weave in ends.

8 Tallinn

Skill level: ❄

With clean lines and rounded petals, this snowflake is reminiscent of a winter blossom.

Materials:
- Thread required: 5.5m (6yd)

Tools:
- 1.75mm crochet hook

Finished diameter: 64mm (2½in)

Foundation ring: ch 6, and join with sl st in first ch. (See Step 1.)

Rnd 1: ch 1 (counts as dc). 11 dc in ring. Join with sl st in initial ch 1. (See Step 1.)

Rnd 2: ch 4 (counts as dtr). dtr in same ch as last sl st. *ch 6, skip 1 dc, and 2 dtr in 1 dc. Repeat from * 4 more times. ch 6, and join with sl st in top of initial ch 4. (See Steps 2–4.)

Rnd 3: *ch 4, and sl st in next dtr. In ch-6 space: [4 tr, ch 8, and sl st in 8th ch from hook to form picot, 4 tr].** sl st in 1 dtr. Repeat from * 4 more times, and from * to ** once. Join with sl st in sl st. Fasten off; weave in ends. (See Steps 5–8.)

Chart key:

- ○ **ch** Chain
- • **sl st** Slip stitch
- + **dc** Double crochet
- ⊤ **tr** Treble crochet
- ⊤ **dtr** Double treble crochet

1 ch 6, and sl st in the first chain to form the foundation ring. ch 1 (this counts as the first dc of Rnd 1). 11 dc in foundation ring. sl st in the ch 1 that began the round.

2 ch 4 (this counts as the first dtr of Rnd 2). dtr in same ch as last sl st (the stitch that joined the last round).

3 *ch 6, skip 1 dc, and 2 dtr in 1 dc.

4 Repeat Step 3 four times. ch 6, and sl st in top of the ch 4 that began the round.

5 *ch 4, and sl st in next dtr.

6 4 tr in ch 6-space. ch 8, and sl st in the eighth ch from hook to form picot.

7 4 tr in same ch-6 space as last tr.** sl st in 1 dtr.

8 Repeat Steps 5–7 four more times. Begin a fifth repeat, but stop when you get to the **. Join with sl st in sl st. Fasten off and weave in ends.

9 Sokcho

Skill level: ❄

This lacy design is created from a simple base of treble crochets, with clusters of chained loops at its points.

Materials:
- Thread required: 5.5m (6yd)

Tools:
- 1.75mm crochet hook

Finished diameter: 70mm (2¾in)

Foundation ring: ch 6, and join with sl st in first ch. (See Step I.)

Rnd I: ch 3 (counts as tr). tr in ring. [ch 4, 2 tr] 5 times in ring. ch 4, and join with sl st in top of initial ch 3. (See Step I.)

Rnd 2: sl st in tr and in ch-4 point. ch 3 (counts as tr). [tr, ch 4, 2 tr] in same ch-4 point. *ch 2, [2 tr, ch 4, 2 tr] in next ch-4 point. Repeat from * 4 more times. ch 2, and join with sl st in initial ch 3. (See Steps 2–4.)

Rnd 3: sl st in tr and in ch-4 point. ch I (counts as dc). 2 dc in same ch-4 point. *ch 6, and sl st in 6th ch from hook to form picot. ch 8, and sl st in 8th ch from hook to form picot. ch 6, and sl st in 6th ch from hook to form picot. 3 dc in same ch-4 point. ch 5.** 3 dc in next ch-4 point. Repeat from * 4 more times, and from * to ** once. Join with sl st in initial ch I. Fasten off; weave in ends. (See Steps 5–8.)

Chart key:

◯ **ch** Chain

• **sl st** Slip stitch

+ **dc** Double crochet

† **tr** Treble crochet

1 ch 6, and sl st in the first chain to form the foundation ring. ch 3 (this counts as the first tr of Rnd I), and tr in ring. [ch 4, 2 tr] five times in ring. ch 4, and sl st in the top of the ch 3 that began the round.

2 sl st in tr, and in ch-4 point. ch 3 (this counts as the first tr of Rnd 2), and [tr, ch 4, 2 tr] in the same ch-4 point.

3 *ch 2. [2 tr, ch 4, 2 tr] in the next ch-4 point.

4 Repeat Step 3 four more times. ch 2, and sl st in top of the ch 3 that began Rnd 2.

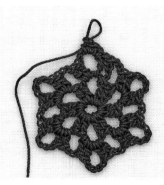

5 sl st in tr, and in ch-4 point. ch I (this counts as the first dc of Rnd 3). 2 dc in the same ch-4 point. .

6 *ch 6, and sl st in the sixth ch from hook to form picot. ch 8, and sl st in the eighth ch from hook to form picot. ch 6, and sl st in the sixth ch from hook to form picot.

7 3 dc in the same ch-4 point as the last dc. ch 5.** 3 dc in the next ch-4 point.

8 Repeat Steps 6 and 7 four more times. Begin a fifth repeat, but stop when you get to the **. sl st in the ch I that began the round. Fasten off and weave in ends.

10 Winnipeg

Skill level: ❄

Winnipeg serves as an introduction to the half-treble crochet stitch, which forms the smooth, firm edges of its base.

Materials:
- Thread required: 5.5m (6yd)

Tools:
- 1.75mm crochet hook

Finished diameter: 76mm (3in)

Foundation ring: ch 6, and join with sl st in first ch. (See Step 1.)

Rnd 1: ch 1 (counts as dc). 11 dc in ring. Join with sl st in initial ch 1. (See Step 1.)

Rnd 2: ch 3 (counts as tr). tr in 1 dc. *ch 7. tr in 2 dc. Repeat from * 4 more times. ch 7, and join with sl st in top of initial ch 3. (See Steps 2–3.)

Rnd 3: ch 2 (counts as htr). *ch 5, and sl st in 5th ch from hook to form picot. htr in next tr. 4 htr in ch-7 space. ch 10, and sl st in 4th ch from hook to form picot. ch 5, and sl st in 1st ch of last ch 10. 4 htr in same ch-7 space as last htr.** htr in 1 tr. Repeat from * 4 more times, and from * to ** once. Join with sl st in top of initial ch 2. Fasten off; weave in ends. (See Steps 3–8.)

Chart key:

  ○ **ch** Chain

  • **sl st** Slip stitch

  + **dc** Double crochet

  ⊤ **htr** Half treble crochet

  ⊤ **tr** Treble crochet

1 ch 6, and sl st in the first chain to form the foundation ring. ch I (this counts as the first dc of Rnd I). II dc in foundation ring. sl st in the ch I that began the round.

2 ch 3 (this counts as the first tr of Rnd 2). tr in I dc. *ch 7. tr in 2 dc. Repeat from * four times.

3 ch 7, and sl st in top of the ch 3 that began the round. ch 2 (this counts as the first htr of Rnd 3).

4 *ch 5, and sl st in the fifth ch from hook to form picot. htr in next tr. 4 htr in ch-7 space.

5 ch I0, and sl st in the fourth ch from hook to form picot.

6 ch 5, and sl st in the first ch of last ch I0.

7 4 htr in the same ch-7 space as the last htr.** htr in I tr.

8 Repeat Steps 4–7 four more times. Begin a fifth repeat, but stop when you get to the **. sl st in the top of the ch 2 that began the round. Fasten off and weave in ends.

11 St Petersburg

Skill level: ❄

This elegant pattern takes its name from a city known for both its stunning architecture and its winter weather.

Materials:
■ Thread required: 9.1m (10yd)

Tools:
■ 1.75mm crochet hook

Finished diameter: 89mm (3½in)

Foundation ring: ch 6, and join with sl st in first ch. (See Step 1.)

Rnd 1: ch 3 (counts as tr). [ch 2, tr] 11 times in ring. ch 2, and join with sl st in top of initial ch 3. (See Steps 1–2.)

Rnd 2: sl st in ch-2 space, and ch 1 (counts as dc). [ch 3, dc] in each of next 11 ch-2 spaces. ch 3, and join with sl st in initial ch 1. (See Steps 2–3.)

Rnd 3: sl st in ch-3 space, and ch 3 (counts as tr), 3 tr in same ch-3 space. 4 tr in each of the 11 remaining ch-3 spaces. Join with sl st in top of initial ch 3. (See Steps 3–4.)

Rnd 4: sl st in 1 tr, and ch 1 (counts as dc). *ch 6, and sl st in 6th ch from hook to form picot. dc in next tr. ch 5. Skip 2 tr, and dtr in 1 tr. ch 9, and sl st in 8th ch from hook to form picot. ch 10, and sl st in 10th ch from hook to form picot. ch 8, and sl st in 8th ch from hook to form picot. sl st in 1st ch of last ch 9 made. dtr in next tr. ch 5.** Skip 2 tr, and dc in 1 tr. Repeat from * 4 more times, and from * to ** once. Join with sl st in initial ch 1. Fasten off; weave in ends. (See Steps 4–8.)

Chart key:

◯ **ch** Chain	• **sl st** Slip stitch	+ **dc** Double crochet	T **tr** Treble crochet	‡ **dtr** Double treble crochet

1 ch 6, and sl st in the first chain to form the foundation ring. ch 3 (this counts as the first tr of Rnd 1). [ch 2, tr] 11 times in ring.

2 ch 2. sl st in the top of the ch 3 that began the round, and in ch-2 space. ch 1 (this counts as the first dc of Rnd 2). [ch 3, dc] in each of next 11 ch-2 spaces.

3 ch 3. sl st in the ch 1 that began the round, and in ch-3 space. ch 3 (this counts as the first tr of Rnd 3). 3 tr in same ch-3 space.

4 4 tr in each of the 11 remaining ch-3 spaces. sl st in the top of the ch 3 that began the round, and in 1 tr. ch 1 (this counts as the first dc of Rnd 4).

5 *ch 6, and sl st in the sixth ch from hook to form picot. dc in next tr. ch 5, skip 2 tr, and dtr in 1 tr.

6 ch 9, and sl st in the eighth ch from hook to form picot. ch 10, and sl st in the tenth ch from hook to form picot. ch 8, and sl st in the eighth ch from hook to form picot.

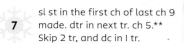
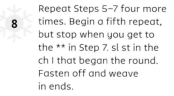

7 sl st in the first ch of last ch 9 made. dtr in next tr. ch 5.** Skip 2 tr, and dc in 1 tr.

8 Repeat Steps 5–7 four more times. Begin a fifth repeat, but stop when you get to the ** in Step 7. sl st in the ch 1 that began the round. Fasten off and weave in ends.

12 Windwhistle

Skill level: ❄

By now, you have probably noticed that many crochet snowflakes begin with a simple hexagonal base, and use a chained border to create decorative points and edges. With practice, you can employ this method to create your own designs.

Materials:
■ Thread required: 8.2m (9yd)

Tools:
■ 1.75mm crochet hook

Finished diameter: 86mm (3⅜in)

Foundation ring: ch 8, and join with sl st in first ch. (See Step 1.)

Rnd 1: ch 4 (counts as dtr). 2 dtr in ring. [ch 3, 3 dtr] 5 times in ring. ch 3, and join with sl st in top of initial ch 4. (See Step 1.)

Rnd 2: ch 4 (counts as dtr). dtr in 2 dtr. *[2 dtr, ch 3, 2 dtr] in ch-3 point.** dtr in 3 dtr. Repeat from * 4 more times, and from * to ** once. Join with sl st in top of initial ch 4. (See Steps 2–4.)

Rnd 3: ch 1 (counts as dc). *ch 4. Skip 1 dtr, and dc in 1 dtr. ch 3. Skip 2 dtr. In ch-3 point, work: [dc, ch 6, tr, ch 10, tr, ch 6, dc]. ch 3. Skip 2 dtr.** dc in 1 dtr. Repeat from * 4 more times, and from * to ** once. Join with sl st in initial ch 1. Fasten off; weave in ends. (See Steps 4–8.)

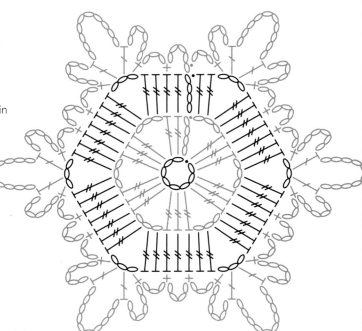

Chart key:

⊙ **ch** Chain

• **sl st** Slip stitch

+ **dc** Double crochet

⊤ **tr** Treble crochet

⊤ **dtr** Double treble crochet

1 ❄ ch 8, and sl st in the first chain to form the foundation ring. ch 4 (this counts as the first dtr of Rnd I). 2 dtr in ring. [ch 3, 3 dtr] five times in ring. ch 3, and sl st in the top of the ch 4 that began the round.

2 ❄ ch 4 (this counts as the first dtr of Rnd 2). dtr in 2 dtr.

3 ❄ *[2 dtr, ch 3, 2 dtr] in ch-3 point.** dtr in 3 dtr.

4 ❄ Repeat Step 3 four more times. Begin a fifth repeat, but stop when you get to the **. sl st in the top of the ch 4 that began the round, and ch I (this counts as the first dc of Rnd 3).

5 ❄ *ch 4. Skip I dtr, and dc in I dtr. ch 3. Skip 2 dtr, and [dc, ch 6, tr] in ch-3 point.

6 ❄ [ch IO, tr, ch 6, dc] in same ch-3 point.

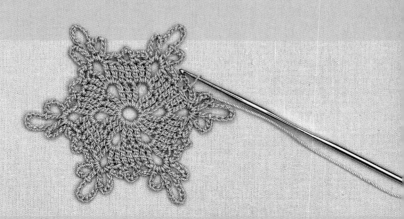

7 ❄ ch 3. Skip 2 dtr.** dc in I dtr.

8 ❄ Repeat Steps 5–7 four more times. Begin a fifth repeat, but stop when you get to the ** in Step 7. sl st in the ch I that began the round. Fasten off and weave in ends.

13 Nuuk

Skill level: ❄

Large, showy and surprisingly easy to make, this snowflake might be at home in Greenland's chilly capital.

Materials:
■ Thread required: 8.2m (9yd)

Tools:
■ 1.75mm crochet hook

Finished diameter: 86mm (3⅜in)

Foundation ring: ch 6, and join with sl st in first ch. (See Step 1.)

Rnd 1: ch 3 (counts as tr). tr in ring. [ch 3, 2 tr] 5 times in ring. ch 3. Join with sl st in top of initial ch 3. (See Step 1.)

Rnd 2: ch 3 (counts as tr). tr in next tr. *[2 tr, ch 9, 2 tr] in ch-3 point.** tr in 2 tr. Repeat from * 4 more times, and from * to ** once. Join with sl st in top of initial ch 3. (See Steps 2–4.)

Rnd 3: ch 1 (counts as dc). *ch 4, and sl st in 4th ch from hook to form picot. dc in 3 tr. ch 6, and tr in top of next ch-9 loop. [ch 8, and sl st in 8th ch from hook to form picot] 3 times. tr in same loop as last tr. ch 6.** dc in 3 tr. Repeat from * 4 more times, and from * to ** once. dc in 2 tr. Join with sl st in initial ch 1. Fasten off; weave in ends. (See Steps 4–8.)

Chart key:

○ **ch** Chain

· **sl st** Slip stitch

+ **dc** Double crochet

┬ **tr** Treble crochet

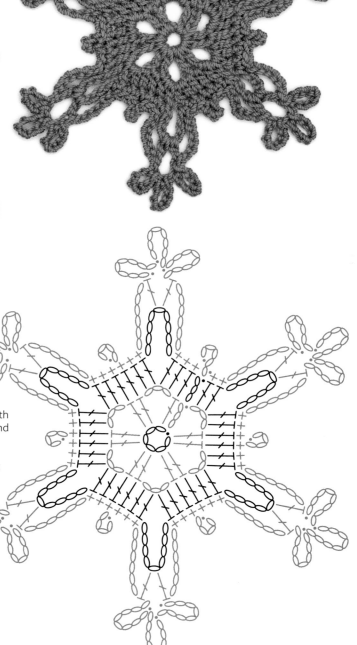

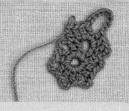

1 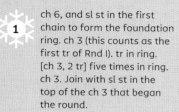 ch 6, and sl st in the first chain to form the foundation ring. ch 3 (this counts as the first tr of Rnd 1). tr in ring. [ch 3, 2 tr] five times in ring. ch 3. Join with sl st in the top of the ch 3 that began the round.

2 ch 3 (this counts as the first tr of Rnd 2). tr in next tr.

3 *[2 tr, ch 9, 2 tr] in ch-3 point.** tr in 2 tr.

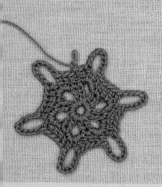
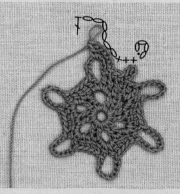

4 Repeat Step 3 four more times. Begin a fifth repeat, but stop when you get to the **. sl st in the top of the ch 3 that began the round, and ch 1 (this counts as the first dc of Rnd 3).

5 *ch 4, and sl st in the fourth ch from hook to form picot. dc in 3 tr. ch 6. tr in top of next ch-9 loop.

6 [ch 8, and sl st in the eighth ch from hook to form picot] three times.

7 tr in same loop as last tr. ch 6.** dc in 3 tr.

8 Repeat Steps 5–7 four more times. Begin a fifth repeat, but stop when you get to the ** in Step 7. dc in 2 tr. sl st in the ch 1 that began Rnd 3. Fasten off and weave in ends.

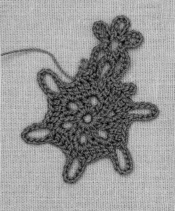
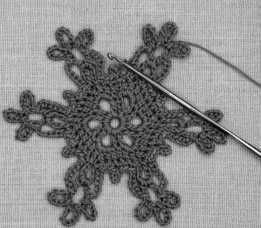
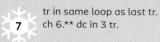

14 Karaj

Skill level: ❄❄

This snowflake features a central star, surrounded by a halo of chain and clusters of loops.

Materials:
■ Thread required: 6.4m (7yd)

Tools:
■ 1.75mm crochet hook

Finished diameter: 76mm (3in)

Foundation ring: ch 6, and join with sl st in first ch. (See Step 1.)

Rnd 1: ch 1 (counts as dc). 11 dc in ring. Join with sl st in initial ch 1. (See Step 1.)

Rnd 2: ch 1 (counts as dc). dc in 1 dc. *ch 8. dc in 2 dc. Repeat from * 4 more times. ch 8, and join with sl st in initial ch 1. (See Step 2.)

Rnd 3: ch 1 (counts as dc). dc in 1 dc. *[4 dc, ch 5, 4 dc] in ch-8 space.** dc in 2 dc. Repeat from * 4 more times, and from * to ** once. Join with sl st in initial ch 1. (See Steps 3–4.)

Rnd 4: sl st in 5 dc, and in ch-5 point. ch 1 (counts as dc). 2 dc in same ch-5 point. *ch 8, and sl st in 8th ch from hook to form picot. ch 10, and sl st in 10th ch from hook to form picot. ch 8, and sl st in 8th ch from hook to form picot. 3 dc in same ch-5 point. ch 5.** 3 dc in next ch-5 point. Repeat from * 4 more times, and from * to ** once. Join with sl st in initial ch 1. Fasten off; weave in ends. (See Steps 5–8.)

Chart key:

⌒ **ch** Chain

• **sl st** Slip stitch

+ **dc** Double crochet

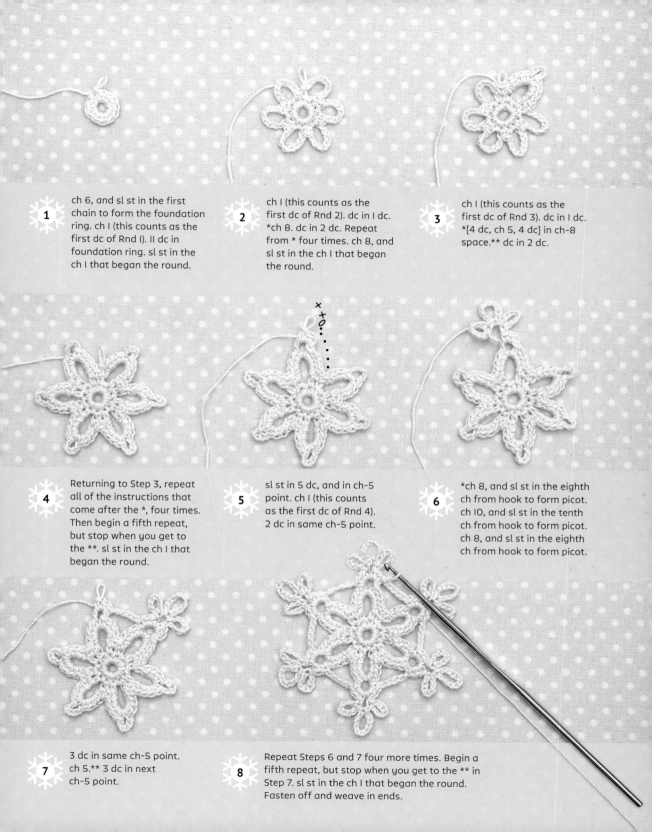

1 ch 6, and sl st in the first chain to form the foundation ring. ch 1 (this counts as the first dc of Rnd 1). 11 dc in foundation ring. sl st in the ch 1 that began the round.

2 ch 1 (this counts as the first dc of Rnd 2). dc in 1 dc. *ch 8. dc in 2 dc. Repeat from * four times. ch 8, and sl st in the ch 1 that began the round.

3 ch 1 (this counts as the first dc of Rnd 3). dc in 1 dc. *[4 dc, ch 5, 4 dc] in ch-8 space.** dc in 2 dc.

4 Returning to Step 3, repeat all of the instructions that come after the *, four times. Then begin a fifth repeat, but stop when you get to the **. sl st in the ch 1 that began the round.

5 sl st in 5 dc, and in ch-5 point. ch 1 (this counts as the first dc of Rnd 4). 2 dc in same ch-5 point.

6 *ch 8, and sl st in the eighth ch from hook to form picot. ch 10, and sl st in the tenth ch from hook to form picot. ch 8, and sl st in the eighth ch from hook to form picot.

7 3 dc in same ch-5 point. ch 5.** 3 dc in next ch-5 point.

8 Repeat Steps 6 and 7 four more times. Begin a fifth repeat, but stop when you get to the ** in Step 7. sl st in the ch 1 that began the round. Fasten off and weave in ends.

15 Munich

Skill level: ❋❋❋

This graceful design displays a pattern of alternating long and short spires.

Materials:
- Thread required: 7.3m (8yd)

Tools:
- 1.75mm crochet hook

Finished diameter: 95mm (3¾in)

Foundation ring: ch 4, and join with sl st in first ch. (See Step 1.)

Rnd 1: ch 4 (counts as dtr). [ch 5, dtr] 5 times in ring. ch 5, and join with sl st in top of initial ch 4. (See Step 1.)

Rnd 2: sl st in next ch-5 space, and ch 4 (counts as dtr). 4 dtr in same ch-5 space. [ch 3, 5 dtr] in each of the 5 remaining ch-5 spaces. ch 3. Join with sl st in top of initial ch 4. (See Step 2.)

Rnd 3: ch 3 (counts as tr). tr in 1 dtr. *In next dtr: [tr, ch 10, and sl st in 8th ch from hook, ch 2, tr]. tr in 2 dtr. ch 16, and sl st in 8th ch from hook to form picot. ch 4. Skip 4 ch, and sl st in 1 ch. ch 3. Skip the remainder of the chain, and skip ch-3 space.** tr in 2 dtr. Repeat from * 4 more times, and from * to ** once. Join with sl st in top of initial ch 3. Fasten off; weave in ends. (See Steps 3–8.)

Chart key:

- ◦ **ch** Chain
- • **sl st** Slip stitch
- ⊤ **tr** Treble crochet
- ⊥ **dtr** Double treble crochet

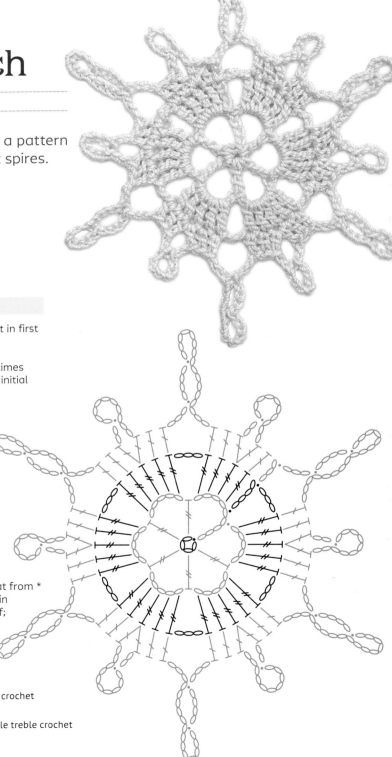

1 ch 4, and sl st in the first chain to form the foundation ring. ch 4 (this counts as the first dtr of Rnd 1). [ch 5, dtr] five times in ring. ch 5, and sl st in the top of the ch 4 that began the round.

2 sl st in next ch-5 space. ch 4 (this counts as the first dtr of Rnd 2). 4 dtr in same ch-5 space. [ch 3, 5 dtr] in each of the five remaining ch-5 spaces. ch 3. sl st in the top of the ch 4 that began the round.

3 ch 3 (this counts as the first tr of Rnd 3). tr in 1 dtr.

4 *In next dtr: [tr, ch 10, and sl st in the eighth ch from hook, ch 2, tr].

5 tr in 2 dtr. ch 16, and sl st in the eighth ch from hook to form picot.

6 ch 4. Skip 4 ch, and sl st in 1 ch.

7 ch 3. Skip the remainder of the chain, and skip ch-3 space.** tr in 2 dtr.

8 Repeat Steps 4–7 four more times. Begin a fifth repeat, but stop when you get to the ** in Step 7. sl st in the top of the ch 3 that began the round. Fasten off and weave in ends.

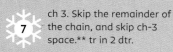

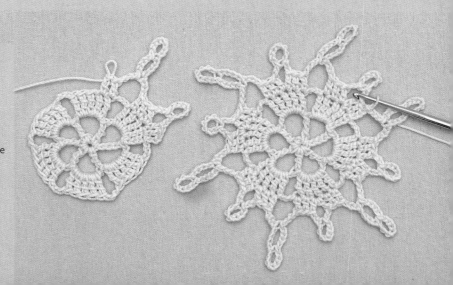

16 Portillo

Skill level: ❄ ❄

The thick curves and sharp points of this crystal could almost have been drawn by a calligraphy pen. They are created by covering long chains with thick layers of double and half-treble crochet.

Materials:
■ Thread required: 9.1m (10yd)

Tools:
■ 1.75mm crochet hook

Finished diameter: 73mm (2⅞in)

Foundation ring: ch 6, and join with sl st in first ch. (See Step I.)

Rnd I: ch I (counts as dc). dc in ring. [ch 8, 2 dc] 5 times in ring. ch 8, and join with sl st in initial ch I. (See Step I.)

Rnd 2: sl st in dc. *[5 dc, ch 3, 5 dc] in ch-8 loop.** sl st in 2 dc. Repeat from * 4 more times, and from * to ** once. Join with sl st in sl st. (See Step 2.)

Rnd 3: sl st in next sl st, in 5 dc, in I ch, and in ch-3 point. ch I (counts as dc). [ch 9, dc] in same ch-3 point. *ch 6. [dc, ch 9, dc] in next ch-3 point. Repeat from * 4 more times. ch 6, and join with sl st in initial ch I. (See Steps 3–5.)

Rnd 4: *[5 dc, ch 3, 5 dc] in ch-9 loop. sl st in dc. [4 htr, ch 3, 4 htr] in ch-6 space.** sl st in dc. Repeat from * 4 more times, and from * to ** once. Join with sl st in sl st. Fasten off; weave in ends. (See Steps 6–8.)

Chart key:

◦ **ch** Chain   + **dc** Double crochet

· **sl st** Slip stitch   ⊤ **htr** Half treble crochet

1 ch 6, and sl st in the first chain to form the foundation ring. ch 1 (this counts as the first dc of Rnd 1). dc in ring. [ch 8, 2 dc] five times in ring. ch 8, and sl st in the ch that began the round.

2 sl st in dc. *[5 dc, ch 3, 5 dc] in ch-8 loop.** sl st in 2 dc. Repeat from * four more times, and from * to ** once. sl st in sl st.

3 sl st in next sl st, in 5 dc, in 1 ch, and in ch-3 point. ch 1 (this counts as the first dc of Rnd 3). [ch 9, dc] in the same ch-3 point.

4 *ch 6. [dc, ch 9, dc] in next ch-3 point.

5 Repeat Step 4 four more times. ch 6, and join with sl st in the ch 1 that began the round.

6 *[5 dc, ch 3, 5 dc] in ch-9 loop. sl st in dc.

7 [4 htr, ch 3, 4 htr] in ch-6 space.** sl st in dc.

8 Repeat Steps 6 and 7 four more times. Begin a fifth repeat, but stop when you get to the ** in Step 7. sl st in sl st. Fasten off and weave in ends.

17 Ben Lomond

Skill level: ❄ ❄

Chains and picots form large diamonds at the points of this design.

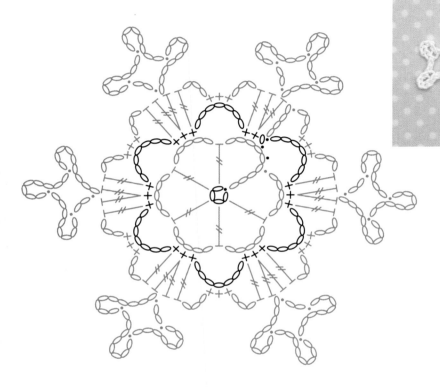

Materials:
- Thread required: 6.4m (7yd)

Tools:
- 1.75mm crochet hook

Chart key:

⌒ **ch** Chain

• **sl st** Slip stitch

+ **dc** Double crochet

╪ **dtr** Double treble crochet

Finished diameter: 86mm (3⅜in)

Foundation ring: ch 4, and join with sl st in first ch. (See Step 1.)

Rnd 1: ch 4 (counts as dtr). [ch 5, dtr] 5 times in ring. ch 5, and join with sl st in initial ch 4. (See Step 1.)

Rnd 2: sl st in 1 ch, and in ch-5 space. ch 1 (counts as dc). 2 dc in same space. [ch 7, 3 dc] in each of the 5 remaining ch-5 spaces. ch 7, and join with sl st in initial ch 1. (See Steps 2–3.)

Rnd 3: ch 4 (counts as dtr). dtr in next dc. *ch 1. [ch 8, and sl st in 6th ch from hook to form picot] 3 times. ch 2. sl st in last ch 1 made. dtr in same dc as last dtr, and in next dc. ch 3. 3 dc in ch-7 space. ch 3.** dtr in 2 dtr. Repeat from * 4 more times, and from * to ** once. Join with sl st in top of initial ch 4. Fasten off; weave in ends. (See Steps 4–8.)

❄ **1** ch 4, and sl st in the first chain to form the foundation ring. ch 4 (this counts as the first dtr of Rnd 1). [ch 5, dtr] five times in ring. ch 5, and sl st in the top of the ch 4 that began the round.

❄ **2** sl st in 1 ch, and in ch-5 space. ch 1 (this counts as the first dc of Rnd 2). 2 dc in same space.

❄ **3** [ch 7, 3 dc] in each of the five remaining ch-5 spaces. ch 7, and sl st in the ch 1 that began the round.

❄ **4** ch 4 (this counts as the first dtr of Rnd 3). dtr in next dc.

❄ **5** *ch 1. [ch 8, and sl st in the sixth ch from hook to form picot] three times.

❄ **6** ch 2. sl st in last ch 1 made.

❄ **7** dtr in same dc as last dtr, and in next dc. ch 3. 3 dc in ch-7 space. ch 3.** dtr in 2 dtr.

❄ **8** Repeat Steps 5–7 four more times. Begin a fifth repeat, but stop when you get to the ** in Step 7. sl st in the top of the ch 4 that began the round. Fasten off and weave in ends.

18 Altay

Skill level: ❄ ❄

This little snowflake looks positively icy, with its smooth edges and sharp points.

Materials:
- Thread required: 6.4m (7yd)

Tools:
- 1.75mm crochet hook

Finished diameter: 64mm (2½in)

Foundation ring: ch 6, and join with sl st in first ch. (See Step 1.)

Rnd 1: ch 3 (counts as tr). 11 tr in ring. Join with sl st in top of initial ch 3. (See Step 1.)

Rnd 2: ch 3 (counts as tr). [ch 2, tr] in each of next 11 tr. ch 2, and join with sl st in top of initial ch 3. (See Step 2.)

Rnd 3: sl st in ch-2 space, and ch 1 (counts as dc). 2 dc in same ch-2 space. *ch 1. 3 dc in next ch-2 space. ch 8, and sl st in 8th ch from hook to form loop.** 3 dc in next ch-2 space. Repeat from * 4 more times, and from * to ** once. Join with sl st in initial ch 1. (See Steps 2–4.)

Rnd 4: sl st in 2 dc, and in ch-1 space. ch 1 (counts as dc). *ch 2. Skip 3 dc, and sl st in next ch (at the base of the ch-8 loop). [dc, 3 htr, ch 3, 3 htr, dc] in ch-8 loop. sl st in next sl st (at the end of the loop). ch 2.** Skip 3 dc, and dc in ch-1 space. Repeat from * 4 more times, and from * to ** once. Join with sl st in initial ch 1. Fasten off; weave in ends. (See Steps 5–8.)

Chart key:

- ◯ **ch** Chain
- • **sl st** Slip stitch
- + **dc** Double crochet
- ⊤ **htr** Half treble crochet
- ⊤ **tr** Treble crochet

1 ch 6, and sl st in the first chain to form the foundation ring. ch 3 (this counts as the first tr of Rnd I). II tr in foundation ring. sl st in the top of the ch 3 that began the round.

2 ch 3 (this counts as the first tr of Rnd 2). [ch 2, tr] in each of next II tr. ch 2, and sl st in the top of the ch 3 that began the round. sl st in ch-2 space, and ch I (this counts as the first dc of Rnd 3). 2 dc in same ch-2 space.

3 *ch I. 3 dc in next ch-2 space. ch 8, and sl st in the eighth ch from hook to form loop.** 3 dc in next ch-2 space.

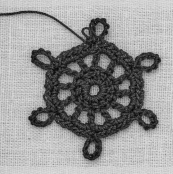

4 Repeat Step 3 four more times. Begin a fifth repeat, but stop when you get to the **. sl st in the ch I that began the round.

5 sl st in 2 dc, and in ch-I space. ch I (this counts as the first dc of Rnd 4).

6 *ch 2. Skip 3 dc, and sl st in next ch (at the base of the ch-8 loop).

7 [dc, 3 htr, ch 3, 3 htr, dc] in ch-8 loop. sl st in next sl st (at the end of the loop). ch 2.** Skip 3 dc, and dc in ch-I space.

8 Repeat Steps 6 and 7 four more times. Begin a fifth repeat, but stop when you get to the ** in Step 7. sl st in the ch I that began the round. Fasten off and weave in ends.

19 Montreal

Skill level: ❄ ❄

Loops of chain filled with double crochet create the feathery edge of this densely patterned crystal.

Materials:
■ Thread required: 6.4m (7yd)

Tools:
■ 1.75mm crochet hook

Finished diameter: 60mm (2⅜in)

Foundation ring: ch 6, and join with sl st in first ch. (See Step I.)

Rnd I: ch I (counts as dc). dc in ring. [ch 3, 2 dc] 5 times in ring. ch 3, and join with sl st in initial ch I. (See Step I.)

Rnd 2: sl st in dc, and in ch-3 space. ch 3 (counts as tr). [tr, ch 2, 2 tr] in same ch-3 space. [2 tr, ch 2, 2 tr] in each of the 5 remaining ch-3 spaces. Join with sl st in top of initial ch 3. (See Steps 2–3.)

Rnd 3: ch I (counts as dc). *ch 2. [dc, ch 8, dc] in next ch-2 point. ch 2. Skip I tr, and dc in I tr. ch 4.** dc in next tr. Repeat from * 4 more times, and from * to ** once. Join with sl st in initial ch I. (See Steps 3–5.)

Rnd 4: sl st in ch-2 space, and ch I (counts as dc). dc in same ch-2 space. *[4 dc, ch 2, 4 dc] in ch-8 loop. 2 dc in ch-2 space. [dc, ch 2, dc] in ch-4 space.** 2 dc in ch-2 space. Repeat from * 4 more times, and from * to ** once. Join with sl st in initial ch I. Fasten off; weave in ends. (See Steps 6–8.)

Chart key:

○ **ch** Chain   + **dc** Double crochet

• **sl st** Slip stitch   ┬ **tr** Treble crochet

 1 ch 6, and sl st in the first chain to form the foundation ring. ch 1 (this counts as the first dc of Rnd 1). dc in ring. [ch 3, 2 dc] five times in ring. ch 3, and join with sl st in the ch 1 that began the round.

 2 sl st in dc, and in ch-3 space. ch 3 (this counts as the first tr of Rnd 2). [tr, ch 2, 2 tr] in same ch-3 space.

 3 [2 tr, ch 2, 2 tr] in each of the five remaining ch-3 spaces. Join with sl st in top of the ch 3 that began the round. ch 1 (this counts as the first dc of Rnd 3).

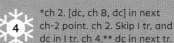 **4** *ch 2. [dc, ch 8, dc] in next ch-2 point. ch 2. Skip 1 tr, and dc in 1 tr. ch 4.** dc in next tr.

5 Repeat Step 4 four more times. Begin a fifth repeat, but stop when you get to the **. sl st in the ch 1 that began the round.

6 sl st in ch-2 space, and ch 1 (this counts as the first dc of Rnd 4). dc in same ch-2 space.

7 *[4 dc, ch 2, 4 dc] in ch-8 loop. 2 dc in ch-2 space. [dc, ch 2, dc] in ch-4 space.** 2 dc in ch-2 space.

8 Repeat Step 7 four more times. Begin a fifth repeat, but stop when you get to the **. sl st in the ch 1 that began the round. Fasten off and weave in ends.

20 Innsbruck

Skill level: ❄ ❄

This small snowflake might be found decorating a street or rooftop in the Austrian city from which it takes its name.

Materials:
■ Thread required: 5.5m (6yd)

Tools:
■ 1.75mm crochet hook

Finished diameter: 60mm (2⅜in)

Foundation ring: ch 6, and join with sl st in first ch. (See Step I.)

Rnd I: ch 3 (counts as tr). tr in ring. [ch 3, 2 tr] 5 times in ring. ch 3, and join with sl st in top of initial ch 3. (See Step I.)

Rnd 2: ch I (counts as dc). dc in tr. *[htr, tr, ch 2, tr, htr] in ch-3 space.** dc in 2 tr. Repeat from * 4 more times, and from * to ** once. Join with sl st in initial ch I. (See Steps I–3.)

Rnd 3: ch I (counts as dc). *ch 2. ch 4, and sl st in 4th ch from hook to form picot. ch 6, and sl st in 6th ch from hook to form picot. ch 4, and sl st in 4th ch from hook to form picot. sl st in 2nd and Ist chains of last ch 2. dc in next dc, in htr, and in tr. In ch-2 point, work: [dc, ch 3, and sl st in 3rd ch from hook, dc].** dc in tr, in htr, and in dc. Repeat from * 4 more times, and from * to ** once. dc in tr, and in htr, and join with sl st in initial ch I. Fasten off; weave in ends. (See Steps 3–8.)

Chart key:

○	**ch** Chain	⊤	**htr** Half treble crochet
•	**sl st** Slip stitch	⊤	**tr** Treble crochet
+	**dc** Double crochet		

1 ch 6, and sl st in the first chain to form the foundation ring. ch 3 (this counts as the first tr of Rnd I). tr in ring. [ch 3, 2 tr] five times in ring. ch 3, and join with sl st in the top of the ch 3 that began the round. ch I (this counts as the first dc of Rnd 2). dc in tr.

2 *[htr, tr, ch 2, tr, htr] in ch-3 space.** dc in 2 tr.

3 Repeat Step 2 four more times. Begin a fifth repeat, but stop when you get to the **. Join with sl st in the ch I that began the round. ch I (this counts as the first dc of Rnd 3).

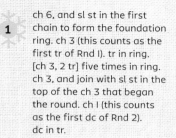

4 *ch 2. ch 4, and sl st in the fourth ch from hook to form picot.

5 ch 6, and sl st in the sixth ch from hook to form picot. ch 4, and sl st in the fourth ch from hook to form picot.

6 sl st in the second and first chains of last ch 2. dc in next dc, in htr, and in tr.

7 In ch-2 point, work: [dc, ch 3, and sl st in the third ch from hook, dc].** dc in tr, in htr, and in dc.

8 Repeat Steps 4–7 four more times. Begin a fifth repeat, but stop when you get to the ** in Step 7. dc in tr, and in htr. sl st in the ch I that began the round. Fasten off and weave in ends.

21 Nome

Skill level: ※ ※

This pattern features a central flower and a serrated outer edge formed from tiny two- and four-chain loops.

Materials:
- Thread required: 6.4m (7yd)

Tools:
- 1.75mm crochet hook

Finished diameter: 64mm (2½in)

Foundation ring: ch 6, and join with sl st in first ch. (See Step I.)

Rnd I: ch 2 (counts as htr). *[ch 2, tr] in ring.** [ch 2, htr] in ring. Repeat from * 4 more times, and from * to ** once. ch 2, and join with sl st in top of initial ch 2. (See Step I–2.)

Rnd 2: sl st in ch-2 space, and ch I (counts as dc). htr in same ch-2 space. *[tr, ch 2, tr] in tr. [htr, dc] in ch-2 space.** [dc, htr] in next ch-2 space. Repeat from * 4 more times, and from * to ** once. Join with sl st in initial ch I. (See Steps 2–4.)

Rnd 3: sl st in htr, in tr, and in ch-2 point. ch I (counts as dc). [ch 6, dc] in same ch-2 point. *ch 6. [dc, ch 6, dc] in next ch-2 point. Repeat from * 4 more times. ch 6, and join with sl st in initial ch I. (See Step 5.)

Rnd 4: sl st in ch-6 loop, and ch I (counts as dc). In the same loop, work: [ch 2, dc, ch 2, dc, ch 4, dc, ch 2, dc, ch 2, dc]. *[3 dc, ch I, 3 dc] in next ch-6 space.** In next ch-6 loop, work: [dc, ch 2, dc, ch 2, dc, ch 4, dc, ch 2, dc, ch 2, dc]. Repeat from * 4 more times, and from * to ** once. Join with sl st in initial ch I. Fasten off; weave in ends. (See Steps 6–8.)

Chart key:

o **ch** Chain

• **sl st** Slip stitch

+ **dc** Double crochet

⊤ **htr** Half treble crochet

⊤ **tr** Treble crochet

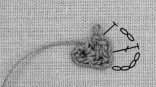

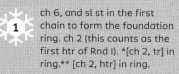

1 ch 6, and sl st in the first chain to form the foundation ring. ch 2 (this counts as the first htr of Rnd I). *[ch 2, tr] in ring.** [ch 2, htr] in ring.

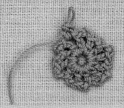

2 Returning to Step I, repeat all of the instructions that come after the *, four more times. Then begin a fifth repeat, but stop when you get to the **. ch 2. sl st in the top of the ch 2 that began the round, and in ch-2 space. ch I (this counts as the first dc of Rnd 2), and htr in same ch-2 space.

3 *[tr, ch 2, tr] in tr. [htr, dc] in ch-2 space.** [dc, htr] in next ch-2 space.

4 Repeat Step 3 four more times. Begin a fifth repeat, but stop when you get to the **. sl st in the top of the ch I that began the round.

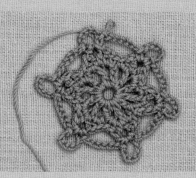

5 sl st in htr, in tr, and in ch-2 point. ch I (this counts as the first dc of Rnd 3). [ch 6, dc] in same ch-2 point. *ch 6. [dc, ch 6, dc] in next ch-2 point. Repeat from * four times. ch 6, and sl st in the ch I that began the round.

6 sl st in ch-6 loop, and ch I (this counts as the first dc of Rnd 4). In the same loop, work: [ch 2, dc, ch 2, dc, ch 4, dc, ch 2, dc, ch 2, dc].

7 *[3 dc, ch I, 3 dc] in next ch-6 space.** In next ch-6 loop, work: [dc, ch 2, dc, ch 2, dc, ch 4, dc, ch 2, dc, ch 2, dc].

8 Repeat Step 7 four times. Begin a fifth repeat, but stop when you get to the **. sl st in the ch I that began the round. Fasten off and weave in ends.

22 Harbin

Skill level: ❅ ❅

Though it is not obvious at first glance, this pattern is a third sibling of St Paul and Minneapolis (see pages 28–31). It is named for Harbin, China, which, serendipitously enough, has a sister city relationship with Minneapolis.

Materials:
■ Thread required: 10.1m (11yd)

Tools:
■ 1.75mm crochet hook

Chart key:

◯ **ch** Chain

• **sl st** Slip stitch

+ **dc** Double crochet

┬ **tr** Treble crochet

‡ **dtr** Double treble crochet

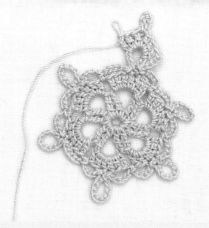
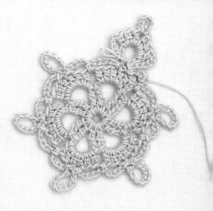

1 To complete the first three rounds of this snowflake, follow Steps 1–8 of St Paul (see page 29). Do not fasten off.

2 *sl st in base of next ch-10 loop. ch 5. In ch-10 loop, work: [3 tr, ch 6, and sl st in the sixth ch from hook, 3 tr].

3 ch 5. sl st in base of same ch-10 loop.

4 ch 5. sl st in next ch-5 space. ch 8, and sl st in the sixth ch from hook to form picot. ch 2. sl st in next ch-5 space. ch 5.

5 Repeat Steps 2–4 five more times. sl st in the sl st that began the round. Fasten off and weave in ends.

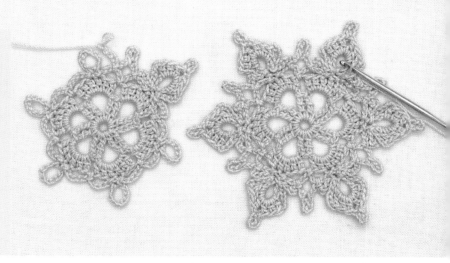

Finished diameter: 89mm (3½in)

Foundation ring: ch 6, and join with sl st in first ch. (See Step 1.)

Rnd 1: ch 4 (counts as dtr). dtr in ring. [ch 5, 2 dtr] 5 times in ring. ch 5, and join with sl st in top of initial ch 4. (See Step 1.)

Rnd 2: sl st in dtr, and in ch-5 space. ch 3 (counts as tr), and 5 tr in same space. *ch 1. 6 tr in next ch-5 space. Repeat from * 4 more times. ch 1,

and join with sl st in top of initial ch 3. (See Step 1.)

Rnd 3: sl st in 2 tr. *ch 10, and sl st in 10th ch from hook to form loop. sl st in next tr. ch 5. Skip 2 tr, and sl st in ch-1 space. ch 5.** Skip 2 tr, and sl st in 1 tr. Repeat from * 4 more times, and from * to ** once . Skip 2 sl st, and join with sl st in sl st. (See Step 1.)

Rnd 4: *sl st in base of next ch-10 loop. ch 5. In ch-10 loop, work: [3 tr, ch 6, and sl st in 6th ch from hook, 3 tr]. ch 5. sl st in base of same ch-10 loop. ch 5. sl st in next ch-5 space. ch 8, and sl st in 6th ch from hook to form picot. ch 2. sl st in next ch-5 space. ch 5. Repeat from * 5 more times. Join with sl st in initial sl st. Fasten off; weave in ends. (See Steps 2–5.)

23 Chrea

Skill level: ※ ※

Africa is not typically associated with snow or skiing, but this delicate design is named after a town, national park and ski resort in the Atlas Mountains of Algeria.

Materials:
- Thread required: 5.5m (6yd)

Tools:
- 1.75mm crochet hook

Finished diameter: 70mm (2¾in)

Foundation ring: ch 6, and join with sl st in first ch. (See Step 1.)

Rnd 1: ch 3 (counts as tr). [ch 2, tr] 11 times in ring. ch 2. Join with sl st in top of initial ch 3. (See Step 1.)

Rnd 2: sl st in ch-2 space, and ch 1 (counts as dc). 2 dc in same space. *[dc, ch 2, dc] in next ch-2 space.** 3 dc in next ch-2 space. Repeat from * 4 more times, and from * to ** once. Join with sl st in initial ch 1. (See Steps 2–4.)

Rnd 3: sl st in 1 dc. *ch 3. Skip 2 dc, and tr in next ch-2 point. ch 6, and sl st in 5th ch from hook to form picot. ch 7, and sl st in 4th ch from hook to form picot. ch 2, and sl st in 1st ch of ch 7. ch 5, and sl st in 5th ch from hook to form picot. sl st in 1st ch of last ch 6. tr in same ch-2 point as last tr. ch 3.** Skip 2 dc, and sl st in 1 dc. Repeat from * 4 more times, and from * to ** once. Skip 1 dc, skip 1 sl st, and sl st in 1 sl st. Fasten off; weave in ends. (See Steps 4–8.)

Chart key:

⌒ **ch** Chain

· **sl st** Slip stitch

+ **dc** Double crochet

⊤ **tr** Treble crochet

 1 ch 6, and sl st in the first chain to form the foundation ring. ch 3 (this counts as the first tr of Rnd I). [ch 2, tr] II times in ring.

 2 ch 2. sl st in the ch 3 that began the round, and in ch-2 space. ch I (this counts as the first dc of Rnd 2). 2 dc in same space.

3 *[dc, ch 2, dc] in next ch-2 space.** 3 dc in next ch-2 space.

4 Repeat Step 3 four more times. Begin a fifth repeat, but stop when you get to the **. sl st in the ch I that began the round, and in I dc.

5 *ch 3. Skip 2 dc, and tr in next ch-2 point. ch 6, and sl st in the fifth ch from hook to form picot. ch 7, and sl st in the fourth ch from hook to form picot. ch 2, and sl st in the first ch of ch 7.

6 ch 5, and sl st in the fifth ch from hook to form picot. sl st in the first ch of last ch 6.

7 tr in same ch-2 point as last tr. ch 3.** Skip 2 dc, and sl st in I dc.

8 Repeat Steps 5–7 four more times. Begin a fifth repeat, but stop at the ** in Step 7. Skip I dc, skip I sl st, and sl st in I sl st. Fasten off and weave in ends.

24 El Serrat

Skill level: ❄ ❄

Layers of double treble crochet create a
solid centre for this large, homely design.

Materials:
- Thread required: 10.1m (11yd)

Tools:
- 1.75mm crochet hook

Chart key:

- ⬯ **ch** Chain
- • **sl st** Slip stitch
- + **dc** Double crochet
- T **dtr** Double treble crochet

Finished diameter: 92mm (3⅝in)

Foundation ring: ch 8, and join with
sl st in first ch. (See Step I.)

Rnd I: ch 4 (counts as dtr). 2 dtr in ring.
[ch 3, 3 dtr] 5 times in ring. ch 3, and
join with sl st in top of initial ch 4.
(See Step I.)

Rnd 2: ch 4 (counts as dtr). dtr in 2 dtr.
*[2 dtr, ch 3, 2 dtr] in ch-3 point.** dtr
in 3 dtr. Repeat from * 4 more times,
and from * to ** once. Join with sl st
in top of initial ch 4. (See Step 2.)

Rnd 3: ch I (counts as dc). *ch 2. dtr in
next dtr. ch 8, and sl st in 6th ch from
hook to form picot. ch 9, and sl st in
9th ch from hook to form picot. ch 6,
and sl st in 6th ch from hook to form
picot. sl st in 2nd and Ist ch of last
ch 8. dtr in same dtr as last dtr. ch 2.
dc in 3 dtr. In next ch-3 space: [2 dc,
ch 9, and sl st in 8th ch from hook to
form picot, ch I, 2 dc].** dc in 3 dtr.
Repeat from * 4 more times, and from
* to ** once. dc in 2 dtr. Join with sl st
in initial ch I. Fasten off; weave in ends.
(See Steps 2–8.)

1 ch 8, and sl st in the first chain to form the foundation ring. ch 4 (this counts as the first dtr of Rnd I). 2 dtr in ring. [ch 3, 3 dtr] five times in ring. ch 3, and sl st in the top of the ch 4 that began the round.

2 ch 4 (this counts as the first dtr of Rnd 2). dtr in 2 dtr. *[2 dtr, ch 3, 2 dtr] in ch-3 point.** dtr in 3 dtr. Repeat from * four more times, and from * to ** once. sl st in the top of the ch 4 that began the round. ch I (this counts as the first dc of Rnd 3).

3 *ch 2. dtr in next dtr. ch 8, and sl st in the sixth ch from hook to form picot.

4 ch 9, and sl st in the ninth ch from hook to form picot. ch 6, and sl st in the sixth ch from hook to form picot.

5 sl st in the second and first ch of last ch 8. dtr in same dtr as last dtr.

6 ch 2. dc in 3 dtr. 2 dc in next ch-3 space. ch 9, and sl st in 8th ch from hook to form picot.

7 ch I. 2 dc in same ch-3 space as last dc.** dc in 3 dtr.

8 Repeat Steps 3–7 four more times. Begin a fifth repeat, but stop when you get to the ** in Step 7. dc in 2 dtr. sl st in the ch I that began the round. Fasten off and weave in ends.

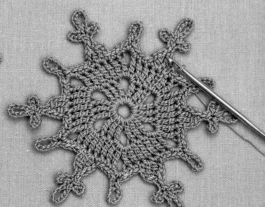

25 Aspen

Skill level: ❄ ❄

This snowflake takes the concept of points made from loop clusters one step further: the points of this snowflake are created from a series of five loops, instead of three.

Materials:
- Thread required:
  7.3m (8yd)

Tools:
- 1.75mm crochet hook

Chart key:

- ○ **ch** Chain
- • **sl st** Slip stitch
- + **dc** Double crochet
- ⊤ **dtr** Double treble crochet

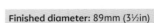

Finished diameter: 89mm (3½in)

Foundation ring: ch 6, and join with sl st in first ch. (See Step 1.)

Rnd 1: ch 4 (counts as dtr). [ch 3, dtr] 11 times in ring. ch 3, and join with sl st in top of initial ch 4. (See Step 1.)

Rnd 2: sl st in 1 ch, and in ch-3 space. ch 1 (counts as dc). [ch 4, dc] in each of 11 remaining ch-3 spaces. ch 4, and join with sl st in initial ch 1. (See Steps 2–3.)

Rnd 3: sl st in ch-4 space, and ch 1 (counts as dc). dc in same ch-4 space. *ch 5, and sl st in 5th ch from hook to form picot. 2 dc in same ch-4 space as last dc. 2 dc in next ch-4 space. ch 10, and sl st in 7th ch from hook to form picot. ch 6, and sl st in 5th ch from hook to form picot. ch 7, and sl st in 7th ch from hook to form picot. ch 5, and sl st in 5th ch from hook to form picot. sl st in 1st ch of last ch 6 made. ch 7, and sl st in 7th ch from hook to form picot. sl st in 3rd, 2nd, and 1st ch of last ch 10. 2 dc in same ch-4 space as last dc.** 2 dc in next ch-4 space. Repeat from * 4 more times, and from * to ** once. Join with sl st in initial ch 1. Fasten off; weave in ends. (See Steps 3–8.)

1 ch 6, and sl st in the first chain to form the foundation ring. ch 4 (this counts as the first dtr of Rnd 1). [ch 3, dtr] 11 times in ring. ch 3, and sl st in the top of the ch 4 that began the round.

2 sl st in 1 ch, and in ch-3 space. ch 1 (this counts as the first dc of Rnd 2). [ch 4, dc] in each of 11 remaining ch-3 spaces. ch 4.

3 sl st in the ch 1 that began the round, and in ch-4 space. ch 1 (this counts as the first dc of Rnd 3), and dc in same ch-4 space.

4 *ch 5, and sl st in the fifth ch from hook to form picot. 2 dc in same ch-4 space as last dc. 2 dc in next ch-4 space.

5 ch 10, and sl st in the seventh ch from hook to form picot. ch 6, and sl st in the fifth ch from hook to form picot. ch 7, and sl st in the seventh ch from hook to form picot. ch 5, and sl st in the fifth ch from hook to form picot.

6 sl st in the first ch of last ch 6 made. ch 7, and sl st in the seventh ch from hook to form picot.

7 sl st in the third, second, and first ch of last ch 10. 2 dc in same ch-4 space as last dc.** 2 dc in next ch-4 space.

8 Repeat Steps 4–7 four more times. Begin a fifth repeat, but stop when you get to the ** in Step 7. sl st in the ch 1 that began the round. Fasten off and weave in ends.

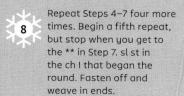

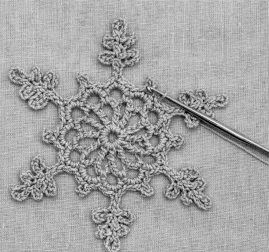

26 Uppsala

Skill level: ❄ ❄

Uppsala's points are constructed much like Aspen's (see pages 66–67), but the more compact centre makes for a smaller, denser finished piece.

Materials:
- Thread required: 6.4m (7yd)

Tools:
- 1.75mm crochet hook

Finished diameter: 70mm (2¾in)

Foundation ring: ch 6, and join with sl st in first ch. (See Step 1.)

Rnd 1: ch 1 (counts as dc). dc in ring. [ch 3, 2 dc] 5 times in ring. ch 3, and join with sl st in initial ch 1. (See Step 1.)

Rnd 2: sl st in dc, and in ch-3 space. ch 3 (counts as tr). [tr, ch 2, 2 tr] in same ch-3 space. [2 tr, ch 2, 2 tr] in each of the 5 remaining ch-3 spaces. Join with sl st in top of initial ch 3. (See Steps 2–3.)

Rnd 3: ch 1 (counts as dc). dc in tr. *2 dc in ch-2 point. ch 7, and sl st in 6th ch from hook to form picot. ch 5, and sl st in 4th ch from hook to form picot. ch 6, and sl st in 6th ch from hook to form picot. ch 4, and sl st in 4th ch from hook to form picot. sl st in 1st ch of last ch 5. ch 6, and sl st in 6th ch from hook to form picot. sl st in 1st ch of last ch 7. 2 dc in same ch-2 point as last 2 dc. dc in 2 tr. ch 4, and sl st in 4th ch from hook.** dc in 2 tr. Repeat from * 4 more times, and from * to ** once. Join with sl st in initial ch 1. Fasten off; weave in ends. (See Steps 3–8.)

Chart key:

- ○ **ch** Chain
- • **sl st** Slip stitch
- + **dc** Double crochet
- T **tr** Treble crochet

1 ch 6, and sl st in the first chain to form the foundation ring. ch I (this counts as the first dc of Rnd I). dc in ring. [ch 3, 2 dc] five times in ring. ch 3, and join with sl st in the ch I that began the round.

2 sl st in dc, and in ch-3 space. ch 3 (this counts as the first tr of Rnd 2). [tr, ch 2, 2 tr] in same ch 3-space.

3 [2 tr, ch 2, 2 tr] in each of the five remaining ch-3 spaces. Join with sl st in top of the ch 3 that began the round. ch I (this counts as the first dc of Rnd 3), and dc in tr.

4 *2 dc in ch-2 point. ch 7, and sl st in the sixth ch from hook to form picot. ch 5, and sl st in the fourth ch from hook to form picot. ch 6, and sl st in the sixth ch from hook to form picot. ch 4, and sl st in the fourth ch from hook to form picot.

5 sl st in the first ch of last ch 5. ch 6, and sl st in the sixth ch from hook to form picot.

6 sl st in the first ch of last ch 7. 2 dc in same ch-2 point as last 2 dc.

7 dc in 2 tr. ch 4, and sl st in the fourth ch from hook to form picot.** dc in 2 tr.

8 Repeat Steps 4–7 four more times. Begin a fifth repeat, but stop when you get to the ** in Step 7. sl st in the ch I that began the round. Fasten off and weave in ends.

27 Dingboche

Skill level: ※ ※ ※ ※

This light and sharp-pointed star is primarily composed of long chains strung with tiny picots.

Materials:
■ Thread required: 6.4m (7yd)

Tools:
■ 1.75mm crochet hook

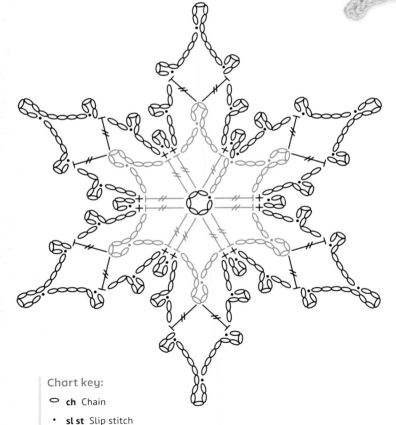

Chart key:

⌒ **ch** Chain

• **sl st** Slip stitch

+ **dc** Double crochet

⊤ **dtr** Double treble crochet

Finished diameter: 89mm (3½in)

Foundation ring: ch 6, and join with sl st in first ch. (See Step I.)

Rnd I: ch 4 (counts as dtr). dtr in ring. *ch 8, and sl st in 5th ch from hook to form loop. ch 3.** 2 dtr in ring. Repeat from * 4 more times, and from * to ** once. Join with sl st in top of initial ch 4. (See Steps I–3.)

Rnd 2: ch I (counts as dc). *ch 4, and sl st in 4th ch from hook to form picot. dc in next dtr. ch 7, and sl st in 4th ch from hook. ch 2. Skip ch-3 space, and dtr in ch-5 loop. ch 4, and sl st in 4th ch from hook to form picot. ch I0, and sl st in 6th ch from hook to form picot. ch 8, and sl st in 4th ch from hook to form picot. dtr in same ch-5 loop as last dtr. ch 6, and sl st in 4th ch from hook to form picot. ch 3. Skip ch-3 space.** dc in dtr. Repeat from * 4 more times, and from * to ** once. Join with sl st in initial ch I. Fasten off; weave in ends. (See Steps 3–8.)

1 ch 6, and sl st in the first chain to form the foundation ring. ch 4 (this counts as the first dtr of Rnd 1). dtr in ring.

2 *ch 8, and sl st in the fifth ch from hook to form loop. ch 3.** 2 dtr in ring.

3 Repeat Step 2 four times. Begin a fifth repeat, but stop when you get to the **. sl st in the ch 4 that began the round, and ch 1 (this counts as the first dc of Rnd 2).

4 *ch 4, and sl st in the fourth ch from hook to form picot. dc in next dtr. ch 7, and sl st in the fourth ch from hook to form picot. ch 2. Skip ch-3 space, and dtr in ch-5 loop.

5 ch 4, and sl st in the fourth ch from hook to form picot. ch 10, and sl st in the sixth ch from hook to form picot. ch 8, and sl st in the fourth ch from hook to form picot. dtr in same ch-5 loop as last dtr.

6 ch 6, and sl st in the fourth ch from hook to form picot. ch 3. Skip ch-3 space.** dc in dtr.

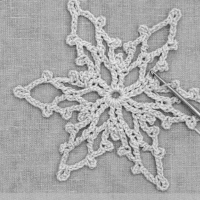

7 Repeat Steps 4–6 four more times.

8 Begin a fifth repeat, but stop when you get to the ** in Step 6. sl st in the ch 1 that began the round. Fasten off and weave in ends.

28 Charlotte Pass

Skill level: ❋❋❋❋

The inner rows of this snowflake are a very basic pattern of treble and double treble crochets, but the design becomes much more exuberant in the outer row, with spreading trios of picot-topped loops.

Materials:
- Thread required: 11m (12yd)

Tools:
- 1.75mm crochet hook

Finished diameter: 102mm (4in)

Foundation ring: ch 4, and join with sl st in first ch. (See Step 1.)

Rnd 1: ch 3 (counts as tr). [ch 3, tr] 5 times in ring. ch 3, and join with sl st in top of initial ch 3. (See Step 1.)

Rnd 2: ch 4 (counts as dtr). *[ch 3, dtr] twice in next ch-3 space.** [ch 3, dtr] in tr. Repeat from * 4 more times, and from * to ** once. ch 3, and join with sl st in top of initial ch 4. (See Step 2.)

Rnd 3: sl st in next ch-3 space, and ch 3 (counts as tr). tr in same space. *[2 tr, ch 6, 2 tr] in 1 ch-3 space.** 2 tr in each of 2 ch-3 spaces. Repeat from * 4 more times, and from * to ** once. 2 tr in next ch-3 space. Join with sl st in top of initial ch 3. (See Step 3.)

Rnd 4: sl st in 2 tr, and ch 1 (counts as dc). dc in 1 tr. *3 dc in ch-6 space. [ch 10, sl st in 4th ch from hook to form picot, ch 5, sl st in 1st ch of last ch 10] 3 times. 3 dc in same ch-6 space as last dc. dc in 2 tr. ch 5.** Skip 4 tr, and dc in 2 tr. Repeat from * 4 more times, and from * to ** once. Join with sl st in initial ch 1. Fasten off; weave in ends. (See Steps 4–8.)

Chart key:

- ⬯ **ch** Chain
- • **sl st** Slip stitch
- + **dc** Double crochet
- ⊤ **tr** Treble crochet
- ⊤ **dtr** Double treble crochet

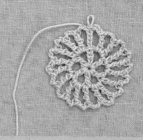

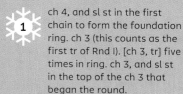

1 ch 4, and sl st in the first chain to form the foundation ring. ch 3 (this counts as the first tr of Rnd 1). [ch 3, tr] five times in ring. ch 3, and sl st in the top of the ch 3 that began the round.

2 ch 4 (this counts as the first dtr of Rnd 2). *[ch 3, dtr] twice in next ch-3 space.** [ch 3, dtr] in tr. Repeat from * four times, and from * to ** once. ch 3, and sl st in the top of the ch 4 that began the round.

3 sl st in next ch-3 space, and ch 3 (this counts as the first tr of Rnd 3). tr in same space. *[2 tr, ch 6, 2 tr] in one ch-3 space.** 2 tr in each of two ch-3 spaces. Repeat from * four times, and from * to ** once. 2 tr in next ch-3 space. sl st in the top of the ch 3 that began the round.

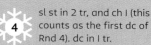

4 sl st in 2 tr, and ch 1 (this counts as the first dc of Rnd 4). dc in 1 tr.

5 *3 dc in ch-6 space. ch 10, and sl st in the fourth ch from hook. ch 5, and sl st in the first ch of last ch 10.

6 [ch 10, sl st in the fourth ch from hook to form picot, ch 5, sl st in the first ch of last ch 10] two more times.

7 3 dc in same ch-6 space as last dc. dc in 2 tr. ch 5.** Skip 4 tr, and dc in 2 tr.

8 Repeat Steps 5–7 four more times. Begin a fifth repeat, but stop when you get to the ** in Step 7. sl st in the ch 1 that began the round. Fasten off and weave in ends.

29 St John's

Skill level: ※ ※ ※ ※

This intricate design gets its name from the colourful and stormy capital of Newfoundland and Labrador, Canada.

Materials:
- Thread required: 11m (12yd)

Tools:
- 1.75mm crochet hook

Chart key:

⬭	**ch**	Chain
•	**sl st**	Slip stitch
+	**dc**	Double crochet
⊤	**tr**	Treble crochet
⊤	**dtr**	Double treble crochet

Finished diameter: 92mm (3⅝in)

Foundation ring: ch 4, and join with sl st in first ch. (See Step I.)

Rnd I: ch 3 (counts as tr). [ch 3, tr] 5 times in ring. ch 3, and join with sl st in top of initial ch 3. (See Step I.)

Rnd 2: sl st in next ch-3 space, and ch 4 (counts as dtr). [2 dtr, ch 10, and sl st in 10th ch from hook, 3 dtr] in same ch-3 space. [3 dtr, ch 10, and sl st in 10th ch from hook, 3 dtr] in each of the next 5 ch-3 spaces. Join with sl st in top of initial ch 4. (See Steps 2–3.)

Rnd 3: ch I (counts as dc). *ch 3. 9 tr in next ch-10 loop. ch 3. Skip 2 dtr, and dc in I dtr. ch 5.** dc in I dtr. Repeat from * 4 more times, and from * to ** once. Join with sl st in initial ch I. (See Steps 3–5.)

Rnd 4: sl st in 3 ch, and in 2 tr. ch I (counts as dc). *ch 4. Skip I tr, and dc in I tr. ch 4. [dc, ch 8, dc] in I tr. [ch 4, dc] in I tr. ch 4, skip I tr, and dc in I tr. ch 2. Skip tr, skip ch-3 space, and skip dc. [dc, ch 6, dc] in ch-5 loop. ch 2.** Skip dc, skip ch-3 space, and skip I tr. dc in I tr. Repeat from * 4 more times, and from * to ** once. Join with sl st in initial ch I. Fasten off; weave in ends. (See Steps 5–8.)

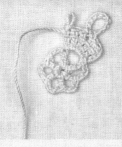

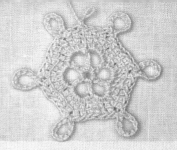

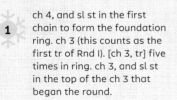

1 ch 4, and sl st in the first chain to form the foundation ring. ch 3 (this counts as the first tr of Rnd I). [ch 3, tr] five times in ring. ch 3, and sl st in the top of the ch 3 that began the round.

2 sl st in next ch-3 space, and ch 4 (this counts as the first dtr of Rnd 2). [2 dtr, ch 10, and sl st in the tenth ch from hook, 3 dtr] in same ch-3 space.

3 [3 dtr, ch 10, and sl st in the tenth ch from hook, 3 dtr] in each of the next five ch-3 spaces. sl st in the top of the ch 4 that began the round, and ch I (this counts as the first dc of Rnd 3).

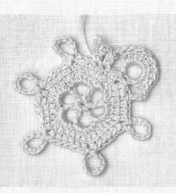

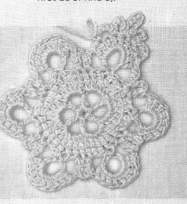

4 *ch 3. 9 tr in next ch-10 loop. ch 3. Skip 2 dtr, and dc in I dtr. ch 5.** dc in I dtr.

5 Repeat Step 4 four more times. Begin a fifth repeat, but stop when you get to the **. sl st in the ch I that began the round, in the next 3 ch, and in 2 tr. ch I (this counts as the first dc of Rnd 4).

6 *ch 4. Skip I tr, and dc in I tr. ch 4. [dc, ch 8, dc] in I tr. [ch 4, dc] in I tr. ch 4, skip I tr, and dc in I tr.

7 ch 2. Skip tr, skip ch-3 space, and skip dc. [dc, ch 6, dc] in ch-5 loop. ch 2.** Skip dc, skip ch-3 space, and skip I tr. dc in I tr.

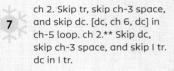

8 Repeat Steps 6 and 7 four more times. Begin a fifth repeat, but stop when you get to the ** in Step 7. sl st in the ch I that began the round. Fasten off and weave in ends.

30 Irkutsk

Skill level: ❄ ❄ ❄

Lacy and light, this ornament would brighten even the darkest winter day.

Materials:
- Thread required: 8.2m (9yd)

Tools:
- 1.75mm crochet hook

Chart key:

○ **ch** Chain

• **sl st** Slip stitch

+ **dc** Double crochet

T **dtr** Double treble crochet

Finished diameter: 89mm (3½in)

Foundation ring: ch 6, and join with sl st in first ch. (See Step I.)

Rnd I: ch I (counts as dc). II dc in ring. Join with sl st in initial ch I. (See Step I.)

Rnd 2: ch 4 (counts as dtr). dtr in same ch as last sl st. *ch 6. Skip I dc. dtr in 2 dc. Repeat from * 4 more times. ch 6, and join with sl st in top of initial ch 4. (See Step 2.)

Rnd 3: *ch 4. sl st in next dtr. ch 5. dtr in ch-6 space. ch 5.** sl st in next dtr. Repeat from * 4 more times, and from * to ** once. Join with sl st in sl st. (See Steps 3–4.)

Rnd 4: sl st in I ch, and in ch-4 point. ch I (counts as dc). *ch 4. Skip ch-5 space, and work in dtr: [dc; ch 9, and sl st in 6th ch from hook to form picot; dtr; ch 6, and sl st in 6th ch from hook to form picot; ch 8, and sl st in 8th ch from hook to form picot; ch 6, and sl st in 6th ch from hook to form picot; dtr; ch 6, and sl st in 6th ch from hook to form picot; ch 3; dc]. ch 4.** Skip ch-5 space, and dc in ch-4 point. Repeat from * 4 more times, and from * to ** once. Join with sl st in initial ch I. Fasten off; weave in ends. (See Steps 4–8.)

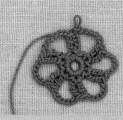

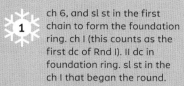

1 ch 6, and sl st in the first chain to form the foundation ring. ch 1 (this counts as the first dc of Rnd 1). 11 dc in foundation ring. sl st in the ch 1 that began the round.

2 ch 4 (this counts as the first dtr of Rnd 2). dtr in same ch as last sl st. *ch 6. Skip 1 dc. dtr in 2 dc. Repeat from * four times. ch 6, and sl st in the top of the ch 4 that began the round.

3 *ch 4. sl st in next dtr. ch 5. dtr in ch-6 space. ch 5.** sl st in next dtr.

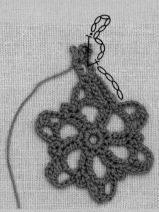

4 Repeat Step 3 four more times. Begin a fifth repeat, but stop when you get to the **. sl st in sl st, in 1 ch, and in ch-4 point. ch 1 (this counts as the first dc of Rnd 4.)

5 *ch 4. Skip ch-5 space, and work the following stitches in the dtr: [dc, ch 9, and sl st in the sixth ch from hook to form picot, dtr].

6 ch 6, and sl st in the sixth ch from hook to form picot. ch 8, and sl st in the eighth ch from hook to form picot. ch 6, and sl st in the sixth ch from hook to form picot.

7 In the last dtr worked in: [dtr, ch 6, and sl st in the sixth ch from hook to form picot, ch 3, dc]. ch 4.** Skip ch-5 space, and dc in ch-4 point.

8 Repeat Steps 5–7 four more times. Begin a fifth repeat, but stop when you get to the ** in Step 7. sl st in the ch 1 that began the round. Fasten off and weave in ends.

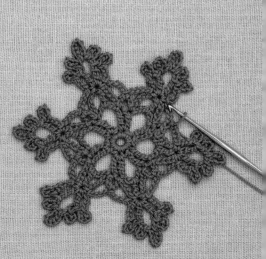

31 Capracotta

Skill level: ❄ ❄ ❄

This fluffy snowflake is named for the Italian town that once reported an astonishing 256cm (101in) of snow in 18 hours.

Materials:
■ Thread required: 9.1m (10yd)

Tools:
■ 1.75mm crochet hook

Chart key:
⬯ **ch** Chain

•   **sl st** Slip stitch

+   **dc** Double crochet

T   **dtr** Double treble crochet

Finished diameter: 92mm (3⅝in)

Foundation ring: ch 6, and join with sl st in first ch. (See Step 1.)

Rnd 1: ch 1 (counts as dc). 11 dc in ring. Join with sl st in initial ch 1. (See Step 1.)

Rnd 2: ch 1 (counts as dc). *ch 10. Skip 1 dc, and dc in 1 dc. Repeat from * 4 more times. ch 10, and join with sl st in initial ch 1. (See Step 2.)

Rnd 3: ch 1 (counts as dc). *ch 6. dtr in ch-10 space. ch 10, and sl st in 10th ch from hook to form loop. dtr in same ch-10 space as last dtr. ch 6.** dc in dc. Repeat from * 4 more times, and from * to ** once. Join with sl st in initial ch 1. (See Steps 3–4.)

Rnd 4: sl st in 6 ch, in dtr, in 1 ch, and in ch-10 loop. ch 1 (counts as dc). dc in same ch-10 loop. *ch 6, and sl st in 6th ch from hook to form picot. dc in same ch-10 loop. ch 7, and sl st in 6th ch from hook to form picot. ch 8, and sl st in 8th ch from hook to form picot. Ch 6, and sl st in 6th ch from hook to form picot. sl st in 1st ch of last ch 7. dc in same ch-10 loop as last dc. ch 6, and sl st in 6th ch from hook to form picot. 2 dc in same ch-10 loop. ch 10, and sl st in 6th ch from hook to form picot. ch 4.** 2 dc in next ch-10 loop. Repeat from * 4 more times, and from * to ** once. Join with sl st in initial ch 1. Fasten off; weave in ends. (See Steps 5–8.)

1 ch 6, and sl st in the first chain to form the foundation ring. ch 1 (this counts as the first dc of Rnd 1). 11 dc in foundation ring. sl st in the ch 1 that began the round.

2 ch 1 (this counts as the first dc of Rnd 2). *ch 10. Skip 1 dc, and dc in 1 dc. Repeat from * four times. ch 10, and sl st in the ch 1 that began the round. ch 1 (this counts as the first dc of Rnd 3).

3 *ch 6. dtr in ch-10 space. ch 10, and sl st in the tenth ch from hook to form loop. dtr in same ch-10 space as last dtr. ch 6.** dc in dc.

4 Repeat Step 3 four more times. Begin a fifth repeat, but stop when you get to the **. sl st in the ch 1 that began the round.

5 sl st in 6 ch, in dtr, in 1 ch, and in ch-10 loop. ch 1 (this counts as the first dc of Rnd 4). dc in same ch-10 loop.

6 *ch 6, and sl st in the sixth ch from hook to form picot. dc in same ch-10 loop. ch 7, and sl st in the sixth ch from hook to form picot. ch 8, and sl st in the eighth ch from hook to form picot. ch 6, and sl st in the sixth ch from hook to form picot. sl st in the first ch of last ch 7.

7 dc in same ch-10 loop as last dc. ch 6, and sl st in the sixth ch from hook to form picot. 2 dc in same ch-10 loop. ch 10, and sl st in the sixth ch from hook to form picot. ch 4.** 2 dc in next ch-10 loop.

8 Repeat Steps 6 and 7 four more times. Begin a fifth repeat, but stop when you get to the ** in Step 7. sl st in the ch 1 that began the round. Fasten off and weave in ends.

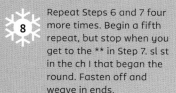

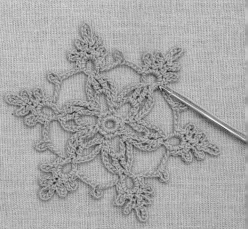

32 Prague

Skill level: ❄ ❄ ❄

With its transparent interior and its wide edge, this pattern is reminiscent of a round window with an ornamental frame.

Materials:
- Thread required: 12.8m (14yd)

Tools:
- 1.75mm crochet hook

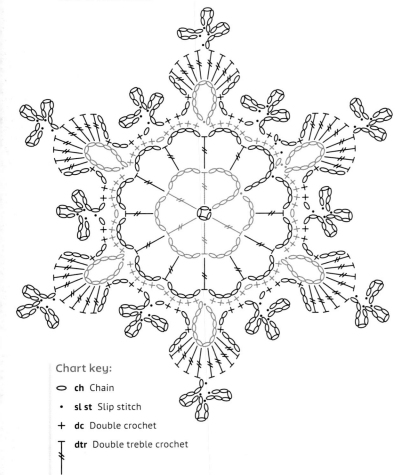

Chart key:

⬭ **ch** Chain

• **sl st** Slip stitch

+ **dc** Double crochet

T **dtr** Double treble crochet

Finished diameter: 108mm (4¼in)

Foundation ring: ch 4, and join with sl st in first ch. (See Step 1.)

Rnd 1: ch 4 (counts as dtr). [ch 5, dtr] 5 times in ring. ch 5, and join with sl st in top of initial ch 4. (See Step 1.)

Rnd 2: ch 4 (counts as dtr). *[ch 5, dtr] in ch-5 space.** [ch 5, dtr] in dtr. Repeat from * 4 more times, and from * to ** once. ch 5, and join with sl st in top of initial ch 4. (See Step 2.)

Rnd 3: sl st in ch-5 space, and ch 1 (counts as dc). 4 dc in same ch-5 space. *ch 1. 5 dc in next ch-5 space. ch 12, and sl st in 12th ch from hook.** 5 dc in next ch-5 space. Repeat from * 4 more times, and from * to ** once. Join with sl st in initial ch 1. (See Steps 2–4.)

Rnd 4: sl st in 2 dc, and ch 1 (counts as dc). dc in next dc. *ch 2. [ch 6, and sl st in 6th ch from hook to form picot] 3 times. sl st in 2nd ch of last ch 2 made. ch 1. Skip 1 dc, skip ch, and skip 1 dc. dc in 2 dc. ch 2. [dc, ch 3, 4 dtr] in next ch-12 loop. ch 1. [ch 6, and sl st in 6th ch from hook to form picot] 3 times. sl st in last ch 1 made. [4 dtr, ch 3, dc] in same ch-12 loop as last dtr. ch 2.** Skip 2 dc. dc in 2 dc. Repeat from * 4 more times, and from * to ** once. Join with sl st in initial ch 1. Fasten off; weave in ends. (See Steps 4–8.)

1 ch 4, and sl st in the first chain to form the foundation ring. ch 4 (this counts as the first dtr of Rnd 1). [ch 5, dtr] five times in ring. ch 5, and sl st in the top of the ch 4 that began the round.

2 ch 4 (this counts as the first dtr of Rnd 2). *[ch 5, dtr] in ch-5 space.** [ch 5, dtr] in dtr. Repeat from * four more times, and from * to ** once. ch 5. sl st in the top of the ch 4 that began the round, and in ch-5 space. ch 1 (this counts as the first dc of Rnd 3). 4 dc in same ch-5 space.

3 *ch 1. 5 dc in next ch-5 space. ch 12, and sl st in 12th ch from hook.** 5 dc in next ch-5 space.

4 Repeat Step 3 four more times. Begin a fifth repeat, but stop when you get to the **. sl st in the ch 1 that began the round, and in 2 dc. ch 1 (this counts as the first dc of Rnd 4), and dc in next dc.

5 *ch 2. [ch 6, and sl st in the sixth ch from hook to form picot] three times. sl st in 2nd ch of last ch 2 made. ch 1. Skip 1 dc, skip ch, and skip 1 dc. dc in 2 dc.

6 ch 2. [dc, ch 3, 4 dtr] in next ch-12 loop. ch 1. [ch 6, and sl st in the sixth ch from hook to form picot] three times. sl st in last ch 1 made.

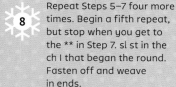

7 [4 dtr, ch 3, dc] in same ch-12 loop as last dtr. ch 2.** Skip 2 dc. dc in 2 dc.

8 Repeat Steps 5–7 four more times. Begin a fifth repeat, but stop when you get to the ** in Step 7. sl st in the ch 1 that began the round. Fasten off and weave in ends.

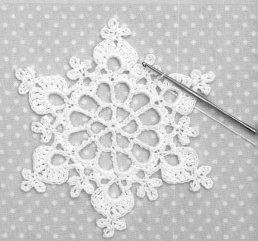

33 Bamiyan

Skill level: ※ ※ ※

A tiny snowflake is suspended in Bamiyan's centre, adding to its varied mix of textures and shapes.

Materials:
- Thread required: 11.9m (13yd)

Tools:
- 1.75mm crochet hook

Chart key:

◯ **ch** Chain

• **sl st** Slip stitch

+ **dc** Double crochet

T **tr** Treble crochet

‡ **dtr** Double treble crochet

Finished diameter: 117mm (4⅝in)

Foundation ring: ch 4, and join with sl st in first ch. (See Step I.)

Rnd I: ch 4 (counts as dtr). *ch 10, and sl st in 8th ch from hook to form picot. ch 2.** dtr in ring. Repeat from * 4 more times, and from * to ** once. Join with sl st in top of initial ch 4. (See Step I.)

Rnd 2: ch 4 (counts as dtr). *ch 12. Skip ch-2 space, skip ch-8 loop, and skip ch-2 space.** dtr in next dtr. Repeat from * 4 more times, and from * to ** once. Join with sl st in top of initial ch 4. (See Step 2.)

Rnd 3: sl st in ch-12 space, and ch I (counts as dc). [ch 5, dc] 5 times in same ch-12 space. [ch 5, dc] 6 times in each of the 5 remaining ch-12 spaces. ch 5, and join with sl st in initial ch I. (See Step 3.)

Rnd 4: sl st in I ch, and in ch-5 space. ch I (counts as dc). dc in same ch-5 space. 2 dc in next ch-5 space. *2 tr in next ch-5 space. ch 3. [ch 8, and sl st in 8th ch from hook to form picot] 5 times. sl st in 3rd and 2nd ch of last ch 3 made. ch I. 2 tr in same ch-5 space as last tr.** 2 dc in each of the next 5 ch-5 spaces. Repeat from * 4 more times, and from * to ** once. 2 dc in each of the 3 remaining ch-5 spaces. Join with sl st in initial ch I. Fasten off; weave in ends. (See Steps 4–8.)

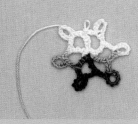

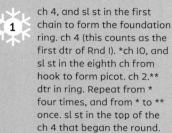

1 ch 4, and sl st in the first chain to form the foundation ring. ch 4 (this counts as the first dtr of Rnd 1). *ch 10, and sl st in the eighth ch from hook to form picot. ch 2.** dtr in ring. Repeat from * four times, and from * to ** once. sl st in the top of the ch 4 that began the round.

2 ch 4 (this counts as the first dtr of Rnd 2). *ch 12. Skip ch-2 space, skip ch-8 loop, and skip ch-2 space.** dtr in next dtr. Repeat from * four times, and from * to ** once. sl st in the top of the ch 4 that began the round.

3 sl st in ch-12 space, and ch 1 (this counts as the first dc of Rnd 3). [ch 5, dc] five times in same ch-12 space. [ch 5, dc] six times in each of the five remaining ch-12 spaces. ch 5, and sl st in the ch 1 that began the round.

4 sl st in 1 ch, and in ch-5 space. ch 1 (this counts as the first dc of Rnd 4). dc in same ch-5 space. 2 dc in next ch-5 space.

5 *2 tr in next ch-5 space. ch 3. [ch 8, and sl st in the eighth ch from hook to form picot] five times.

6 sl st in the third and second ch of last ch 3 made. ch 1. 2 tr in same ch-5 space as last tr.**

7 2 dc in each of the next five ch-5 spaces.

8 Repeat Steps 5–7 four more times. Begin a fifth repeat, but stop when you get to the ** in Step 6. 2 dc in each of the three remaining ch-5 spaces. sl st in the ch 1 that began the round. Fasten off and weave in ends.

34 Caribou

Skill level: ✳ ✳ ✳

Chains and slip stitches sketch an elegant pattern of loops and arms around the periphery of this gorgeous design.

Materials:
- Thread required: 9.1m (10yd)

Tools:
- 1.75mm crochet hook

Chart key:

○ **ch** Chain

• **sl st** Slip stitch

+ **dc** Double crochet

ꓕ **tr** Treble crochet

ꓕ **dtr** Double treble crochet

Finished diameter: 89mm (3½in)

Foundation ring: ch 6, and join with sl st in first ch. (See Step 1.)

Rnd 1: ch 4 (counts as dtr). [ch 3, dtr] 11 times in ring. ch 3, and join with sl st in initial ch 4. (See Step 1.)

Rnd 2: sl st in ch-3 space, and ch 3 (counts as tr). 2 tr in same ch-3 space. *[2 tr, ch 2, 2 tr] in next ch-3 space.** 3 tr in next ch-3 space. Repeat from * 4 more times, and from * to ** once. Join with sl st in top of initial ch 3. (See Steps 1–3.)

Rnd 3: sl st in 1 dtr. ch 1 (counts as dc). *ch 9, and sl st in 4th ch from hook to form picot. ch 6, and sl st in 6th ch from hook to form picot. ch 8, and sl st in 8th ch from hook to form picot. ch 6, and sl st in 6th ch from hook to form picot. ch 4, and sl st in 4th ch from hook to form picot. sl st in 5th ch of last ch 9 made. ch 3. sl st in 1st ch of ch 9. dc in last dtr worked in. ch 3. In next ch-2 point, work: [2 tr, ch 10, and sl st in 8th ch from hook to form picot, ch 2, 2 tr]. ch 3.** Skip 3 dtr, and dc in 1 dtr. Repeat from * 4 more times, and from * to ** once. Join with sl st in initial ch 1. Fasten off; weave in ends. (See Steps 3–8.)

1 ch 6, and sl st in the first chain to form the foundation ring. ch 4 (this counts as the first dtr of Rnd I). [ch 3, dtr] II times in ring. ch 3. sl st in the top of the ch 4 that began the round, and in ch-3 space. ch 3 (this counts as the first tr of Rnd 2). 2 tr in same ch-3 space.

2 *[2 tr, ch 2, 2 tr] in next ch-3 space.** 3 tr in next ch-3 space.

3 Repeat Step 2 four more times. Begin a fifth repeat, but stop when you get to the **. sl st in the top of the ch 3 that began the round, and in I dtr. ch I (this counts as the first dc of Rnd 3).

4 *ch 9, and sl st in the fourth ch from hook to form picot.

5 ch 6, and sl st in the sixth ch from hook to form picot. ch 8, and sl st in the eighth ch from hook to form picot. ch 6, and sl st in the sixth ch from hook to form picot. ch 4, and sl st in the fourth ch from hook to form picot.

6 sl st in the fifth ch of last ch 9 made. ch 3. sl st in the first ch of of ch 9. dc in last dtr worked in.

7 ch 3. In next ch-2 point, work: [2 tr, ch I0, and sl st in the eighth ch from hook to form picot, ch 2, 2 tr]. ch 3.** Skip 3 dtr, and dc in I dtr.

8 Repeat Steps 4–7 four more times. Begin a fifth repeat, but stop when you get to the ** in Step 7. sl st in the ch I that began the round. Fasten off and weave in ends.

35 Erzurum

Skill level: ❄ ❄ ❄

With many snowflake patterns, the base is simple and the outer edges create complexity and interest. In this pattern, the opposite is true: the outer edge provides a simple frame for the tiny crystal at the snowflake's centre.

Materials:
- Thread required: 11m (12yd)

Tools:
- 1.75mm crochet hook

Finished diameter: 92mm (3⅝in)

Foundation ring: ch 6, and join with sl st in first ch. (See Step 1.)

Rnd 1: ch 3 (counts as tr). tr in ring. [ch 2, 2 tr] 5 times in ring. ch 2, and join with sl st in top of initial ch 3. (See Step 1.)

Rnd 2: ch 1 (counts as dc). *ch 6, and sl st in 4th ch from hook to form picot. ch 5, and sl st in 5th ch from hook to form picot. ch 4, and sl st in 4th ch from hook to form picot. sl st in 2nd and 1st ch of last ch 6. dc in next tr. 3 dc in ch-2 space.** dc in 1 tr. Repeat from * 4 more times, and from * to ** once. Join with sl st in initial ch 1. (See Steps 1–3.)

Rnd 3: sl st in 6 ch, in sl st, in 2 ch, and in ch-5 loop. ch 1 (counts as dc). *ch 12, and sl st in 12th ch from hook. dc in same ch-5 loop as last dc. ch 8.** dc in next ch-5 loop (at top of next loop cluster). Repeat from * 4 more times, and from * to ** once. Join with sl st in initial ch 1. (See Steps 4–6.)

Rnd 4: sl st in next ch, and in ch-12 loop. ch 2 (counts as htr). 2 htr in same loop. *[ch 3, htr] 3 times in same loop. ch 6. [htr, ch 3] 3 times in same loop. 3 htr in same loop. 6 tr in next ch-8 space.** 3 htr in next ch-12 loop. Repeat from * 4 times, and from * to ** once. Join with sl st in top of initial ch 2. Fasten off; weave in ends. (See Steps 6–8.)

Chart key:

- ◯ **ch** Chain
- • **sl st** Slip stitch
- ＋ **dc** Double crochet
- ⊤ **htr** Half treble crochet
- ⊤ **tr** Treble crochet

1 ch 6, and sl st in the first chain to form the foundation ring. ch 3 (this counts as the first tr of Rnd I). tr in ring. [ch 2, 2 tr] five times in ring. ch 2, and join with sl st in the top of the ch 3 that began the round. ch I (this counts as the first dc of Rnd 2).

2 *ch 6, and sl st in the fourth ch from hook to form picot. ch 5, and sl st in the fifth ch from hook to form picot. ch 4, and sl st in the fourth ch from hook to form picot. sl st in the second and the first ch of last ch 6. dc in next tr. 3 dc in ch-2 space.** dc in I tr.

3 Repeat Step 2 four more times. Begin a fifth repeat, but stop when you get to the **. sl st in the ch I that began the round.

4 sl st in 6 ch, in sl st, in 2 ch, and in ch-5 loop. ch I (this counts as the first dc of Rnd 3).

5 *ch I2, and sl st in I2th ch from hook. dc in same ch-5 loop as last dc. ch 8.** dc in next ch-5 loop (at the top of the next loop cluster).

6 Repeat Step 5 four more times. Begin a fifth repeat, but stop when you get to the **. sl st in the ch I that began the round, in next ch, and in ch-I2 loop. ch 2 (this counts as the first htr of Rnd 4). 2 htr in same loop.

7 *[ch 3, htr] three times in same loop. ch 6. [htr, ch 3] three times in same loop. 3 htr in same loop. 6 tr in next ch-8 space.** 3 htr in next ch-I2 loop.

8 Repeat Step 7 four times. Begin a fifth repeat, but stop when you get to the **. sl st in the top of the ch 2 that began the round. Fasten off and weave in ends.

36 Kiev

Skill level: ※ ※ ※

Long arms and an airy interior give Kiev an appearance of lightness and fragility.

Materials:
- Thread required: 7.3m (8yd)

Tools:
- 1.75mm crochet hook

Chart key:

- ⬭ **ch** Chain
- • **sl st** Slip stitch
- + **dc** Double crochet
- ⊤ **tr** Treble crochet
- ⊤ **dtr** Double treble crochet

Finished diameter: 92mm (3⅝in)

Foundation ring: ch 6, and join with sl st in first ch. (See Step I.)

Rnd I: ch I (counts as dc). II dc in ring. Join with sl st in initial ch I. (See Step I.)

Rnd 2: ch 4 (counts as dtr). *ch 6. Skip I dc, and dtr in I dc. Repeat from * 4 more times. ch 6, and join with sl st in top of initial ch 4. (See Step I.)

Rnd 3: ch 3 (counts as tr). tr in same ch as last sl st. *ch 9, and sl st in 7th ch from hook to form picot. ch II, and sl st in I0th ch from hook to form picot. ch 2. [ch 6, and sl st in 6th ch from hook to form picot] 3 times. sl st in 2nd and Ist ch of last ch 2 made. ch I0, and sl st in I0th ch from hook to form picot. sl st in Ist ch of last ch II made. ch 7, and sl st in 7th ch from hook to form picot. sl st in 2nd and Ist ch of last ch 9 made (these are the two ch at the bottom of this arm). 2 tr in same stitch as last tr. ch 3. sl st in next ch-6 space. ch 3.** 2 tr in next dtr. Repeat from * 4 more times, and from * to ** once. Join with sl st in top of initial ch 3. Fasten off; weave in ends. (See Steps 2–8.)

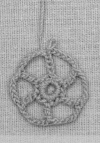

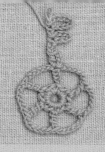

1 ch 6, and sl st in the first chain to the form foundation ring. ch 1 (this counts as the first dc of Rnd 1). 11 dc in foundation ring. sl st in the ch 1 that began the round. ch 4 (this counts as the first dtr of Rnd 2). *ch 6. Skip 1 dc, and dtr in 1 dc. Repeat from * four times. ch 6, and sl st in the top of the ch 4 that began the round.

2 ch 3 (this counts as the first tr of Rnd 3). tr in same ch as last sl st.

3 *ch 9, and sl st in the seventh ch from hook to form picot. ch 11, and sl st in the tenth ch from hook to form picot.

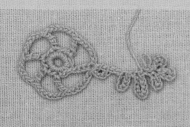

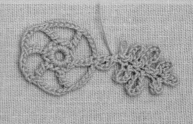

4 ch 2. [ch 6, and sl st in the sixth ch from hook to form picot] three times. sl st in the second and the first ch of last ch 2 made.

5 ch 10, and sl st in the tenth ch from hook to form picot. sl st in the first ch of last ch 11 made.

6 ch 7, and sl st in the seventh ch from hook to form picot. sl st in the second and first ch of last ch 9 made (these are the two ch at the bottom of this arm).

7 2 tr in same stitch as last tr. ch 3. sl st in next ch-6 space. ch 3.** 2 tr in next dtr.

8 Repeat Steps 3–7 four more times. Begin a fifth repeat, but stop when you get to the ** in Step 7. sl st in the top of the ch 3 that began the round. Fasten off and weave in ends.

37 Helsinki

Skill level: ✳ ✳ ✳

Like many snowflake designs, this one is much less complicated than it looks: the ornate edge is formed by repeating a series of identical loop clusters.

Materials:
■ Thread required: 11m (12yd)

Tools:
■ 1.75mm crochet hook

Chart key:

○ **ch** Chain

• **sl st** Slip stitch

+ **dc** Double crochet

⊤ **tr** Treble crochet

Finished diameter: 95mm (3¾in)

Foundation ring: ch 6, and join with sl st in first ch. (See Step I.)

Rnd I: ch I (counts as dc). II dc in ring. Join with sl st in initial ch I. (See Step I.)

Rnd 2: ch I (counts as dc). *[tr, ch 6, tr] in I dc.** dc in I dc. Repeat from * 4 more times, and from * to ** once. Join with sl st in initial ch I. (See Step I.)

Rnd 3: sl st in tr, and in ch-6 space. ch I (counts as dc). [2 dc, ch 4, 3 dc] in same ch-6 space. *ch 2. [3 dc, ch 4, 3 dc] in next ch-6 space. Repeat from * 4 more times. ch 2, and join with sl st in initial ch I. (See Steps 2–3.)

Rnd 4: ch I (counts as dc). dc in 2 dc. *ch 3. tr in ch-4 point. **ch 2. ch 6, and sl st in 6th ch from hook to form picot. ch 8, and sl st in 8th ch from hook to form picot. ch 10, and sl st in 10th ch from hook to form picot. ch 8, and sl st in 8th ch from hook to form picot. ch 6, and sl st in 6th ch from hook to form picot. sl st in 2nd and Ist ch of last ch 2.*** sl st in top of last tr made. ch 3. dc in 3 dc, and in ch-2 space. Repeat from ** to ***. dc in same ch-2 space as last dc.**** dc in 3 dc. Repeat from * 4 more times, and from * to **** once . Join with sl st in initial ch I. Fasten off; weave in ends. (See Steps 3–8.)

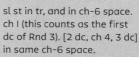

1 ch 6, and sl st in the first chain to form the foundation ring. ch 1 (this counts as the first dc of Rnd 1). 11 dc in foundation ring. sl st in the ch 1 that began the round. ch 1 (this counts as the first dc of Rnd 2). *[tr, ch 6, tr] in 1 dc.** dc in 1 dc. Repeat from * four times, and from * to ** once. sl st in the ch 1 that began the round.

2 sl st in tr, and in ch-6 space. ch 1 (this counts as the first dc of Rnd 3). [2 dc, ch 4, 3 dc] in same ch-6 space.

3 *ch 2. [3 dc, ch 4, 3 dc] in next ch-6 space. Repeat from * 4 times. ch 2, and sl st in the ch 1 that began the round. ch 1 (this counts as the first dc of Rnd 4), and dc in 2 dc.

4 *ch 3. tr in ch-4 point.

5 **ch 2. ch 6, and sl st in the sixth ch from hook to form picot. ch 8, and sl st in the eighth ch from hook to form picot. ch 10, and sl st in the tenth ch from hook to form picot. ch 8, and sl st in the eighth ch from hook to form picot. ch 6, and sl st in the sixth ch from hook to form picot. sl st in the second and first ch of last ch 2.***

6 sl st in top of last tr made. ch 3. dc in 3 dc, and in ch-2 space.

7 Repeat Step 5. dc in same ch-2 space as last dc.**** dc in 3 dc.

8 Repeat Steps 4–7 four more times. Begin a fifth repeat, but stop when you get to the **** in Step 7. sl st in the ch 1 that began the round. Fasten off and weave in ends.

38 Syracuse

Skill level: ✳ ✳ ✳

Long spires cling like icicles to the periphery of this delicate snowflake.

Materials:
■ Thread required: 10.1m (11yd)

Tools:
■ 1.75mm crochet hook

Finished diameter: 121mm (4¾in)

Foundation ring: ch 6, and join with sl st in first ch. (See Step I.)

Rnd I: ch I (counts as dc). II dc in ring. Join with sl st in initial dc. (See Step I.)

Rnd 2: ch 4 (counts as dtr). dtr in same ch as last sl st. *ch 8. Skip I dc, and 2 dtr in I dc. Repeat from * 4 more times. ch 8, and join with sl st in top of initial ch 4. (See Step I.)

Rnd 3: ch I (counts as dc). dc in dtr. *ch 5. dtr in ch-8 space. ch II. sl st in 7th ch from hook. ch 3. sl st in Ist ch of ch II. dtr in same ch-8 space as last dtr. ch 5.** dc in 2 dtr. Repeat from * 4 more times, and from * to ** once. Join with sl st in initial ch I. (See Steps I–4.)

Rnd 4: *ch I5. sl st in 7th ch from hook to form picot. ch 3, and sl st in 5th ch of ch I5. ch 3. sl st in Ist ch of ch I5, and in next dc. ch 8. Skip ch-5 space, and dc in next ch-3 space. ch 5, and dc in ch-7 loop. ch II, and sl st in 7th ch from hook to form picot. ch 3, and sl st in Ist ch of ch II. dc in same ch-7 loop as last dc. ch 5, and dc in next ch-3 space. ch 8. Skip ch-5 space.** sl st in I dc. Repeat from * 4 more times, and from * to ** once. Join with sl st in sl st. Fasten off; weave in ends. (See Steps 5–8.)

Chart key:

⟳ **ch** Chain

· **sl st** Slip stitch

+ **dc** Double crochet

⊤ **dtr** Double treble crochet

1 ch 6, and sl st in the first chain to form the foundation ring. ch I (this counts as the first dc of Rnd I). II dc in foundation ring. sl st in the ch I that began the round. ch 4 (this counts as the first dtr of Rnd 2). dtr in same ch as last sl st. *ch 8. Skip I dc, and 2 dtr in I dc. Repeat from

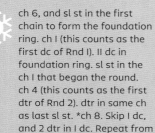
* four times. ch 8, and sl st in the top of the ch 4 that began the round. ch I (this counts as the first dc of Rnd 3). dc in dtr.

2 *ch 5. dtr in ch-8 space. ch II. sl st in the seventh ch from hook.

3 ch 3. sl st in the first ch of ch II. dtr in same ch-8 space as last dtr. ch 5.** dc in 2 dtr.

4 Repeat Steps 2 and 3 four more times. Begin a fifth repeat, but stop when you get to the ** in Step 3. sl st in the ch I that began the round.

5 *ch I5. sl st in the seventh ch from hook to form picot. ch 3, and sl st in the fifth ch of ch I5. ch 3. sl st in the first ch of ch I5, and in next dc.

6 ch 8. Skip ch-5 space, and dc in next ch-3 space. ch 5, and dc in ch-7 loop.

7 ch II, and sl st in the seventh ch from hook to form picot. ch 3, and sl st in the first ch of ch II. dc in same ch-7 loop as last dc. ch 5, and dc in next ch-3 space. ch 8. Skip ch-5 space.** sl st in I dc.

8 Repeat Steps 5–7 four more times. Begin a fifth repeat, but stop when you get to the ** in Step 7. sl st in sl st. Fasten off and weave in ends.

39 Hammerfest

Skill level: ❄ ❄ ❄

Very large and light as gossamer, this snowflake is mostly created from a combination of long chains and the spaces between them.

Materials:
- Thread required: 8.2m (9yd)

Tools:
- 1.75mm crochet hook

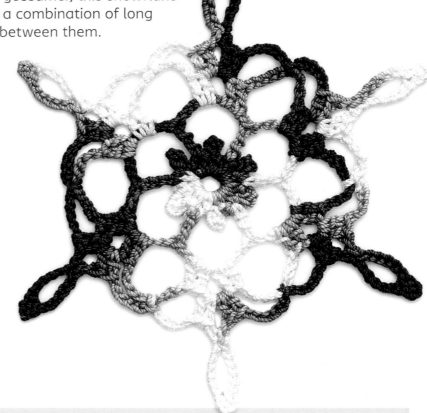

Finished diameter: 108mm (4¼in)

Foundation ring: ch 6, and join with sl st in first ch. (See Step 1.)

Rnd 1: ch 1 (counts as dc). *[ch 2, dc] in ring. ch 4, and sl st in 4th ch from hook to form picot.** dc in ring. Repeat from * 4 more times, and from * to ** once. Join with sl st in initial ch 1. (See Steps 1–2.)

Rnd 2: sl st in ch-2 point, and ch 4 (counts as dtr). *ch 8. Skip dc, skip ch-4 loop, and skip dc. dtr in next ch-2 point. Repeat from * 4 more times. ch 8, and join with sl st in top of initial ch 4. (See Step 3.)

Rnd 3: sl st in 3 ch, and in ch-8 space. ch 3 (counts as tr). [tr, ch 2, 2 tr] in same space. *ch 10. [2 tr, ch 2, 2 tr] in next ch-8 space. Repeat from * 4 more times. ch 10, and join with sl st in top of initial ch 3. (See Step 4.)

Rnd 4: sl st in tr, and in ch-2 point. ch 3 (counts as tr). tr in same point. *ch 12. sl st in 4th ch from hook to form picot. ch 5. sl st in 3rd and 2nd ch of last ch 12. ch 1. 2 tr in same ch-2 space as last tr. ch 6. sl st in ch-10 space. ch 6.** 2 tr in next ch-2 point. Repeat from * 4 more times, and from * to ** once. Join with sl st in top of initial ch 3. Fasten off; weave in ends. (See Steps 5–8.)

Chart key:

- ⬭ **ch** Chain
- ·   **sl st** Slip stitch
- +   **dc** Double crochet
- ⊤   **tr** Treble crochet
- ⊤⧸ **dtr** Double treble crochet

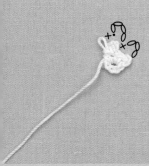

1 ch 6, and sl st in the first chain to form the foundation ring. ch I (this counts as the first dc of Rnd I). *[ch 2, dc] in ring. ch 4, and sl st in the fourth ch from hook to form picot.** dc in ring.

2 Returning to Step I, repeat all of the instructions that come after the *, four times. Then begin a fifth repeat, but stop when you get to the **. sl st in the ch I that began the round.

3 sl st in ch-2 point, and ch 4 (this counts as the first dtr of Rnd 2). *ch 8. Skip dc, skip ch-4 loop, and skip dc. dtr in next ch-2 point. Repeat from * four times. ch 8, and sl st in the top of the ch 4 that began the round.

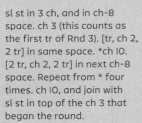

 4 sl st in 3 ch, and in ch-8 space. ch 3 (this counts as the first tr of Rnd 3). [tr, ch 2, 2 tr] in same space. *ch 10. [2 tr, ch 2, 2 tr] in next ch-8 space. Repeat from * four times. ch 10, and join with sl st in top of the ch 3 that began the round.

5 sl st in tr, and in ch-2 point. ch 3 (this counts as tr). tr in same point.

6 *ch 12. sl st in the fourth ch from hook to form picot. ch 5. sl st in the third and the second ch of last ch 12.

7 ch 1. 2 tr in same ch-2 space as last tr. ch 6. sl st in ch-10 space. ch 6.** 2 tr in next ch-2 point.

 8 Repeat Steps 6 and 7 four times. Then begin a fifth repeat, but stop when you get to the ** in Step 7. sl st in the top of the ch 3 that began the round. Fasten off and weave in ends.

40 San Martin

Skill level: ❄ ❄ ❄

Large, intricately patterned and dripping with picots, this star is perfect for winter decorating.

Materials:
■ Thread required: 11.9m (13yd)

Tools:
■ 1.75mm crochet hook

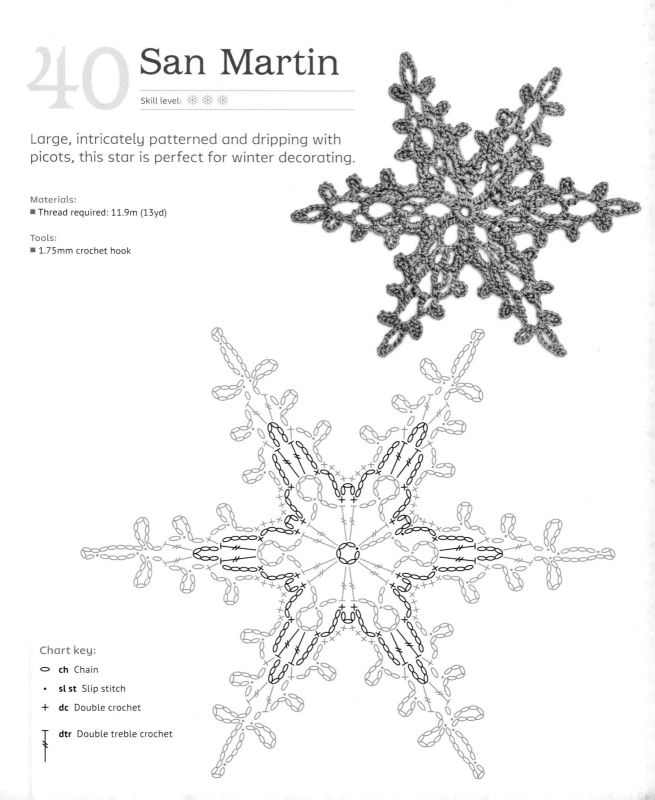

Chart key:

◯ **ch** Chain

• **sl st** Slip stitch

+ **dc** Double crochet

T **dtr** Double treble crochet

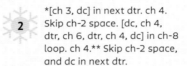

1 ch 6, and sl st in the first chain to form the foundation ring. ch 4 (this counts as the first dtr of Rnd 1). dtr in ring. *ch 10, and sl st in the eighth ch from hook to form loop. ch 2.** 2 dtr in ring. Repeat from * 4 more times, and from * to ** once. sl st in the top of the ch 4 that began the round. ch 1 (this counts as the first dc of Rnd 2).

2 *[ch 3, dc] in next dtr. ch 4. Skip ch-2 space. [dc, ch 4, dtr, ch 6, dtr, ch 4, dc] in ch-8 loop. ch 4.** Skip ch-2 space, and dc in next dtr.

3 Repeat Step 2 four more times. Begin a fifth repeat, but stop when you get to the **. sl st in the ch 1 that began the round, and in the next ch-3 space. ch 1 (this counts as the first dc of Rnd 3), and dc in same ch-3 space.

Finished diameter: 121mm (4¾in)

Foundation ring: ch 6, and join with sl st in first ch. (See Step 1.)

Rnd 1: ch 4 (counts as dtr). dtr in ring. *ch 10, and sl st in 8th ch from hook to form loop. ch 2.** 2 dtr in ring. Repeat from * 4 more times, and from * to ** once. Join with sl st in top of initial ch 4. (See Step 1.)

Rnd 2: ch 1 (counts as dc). *[ch 3, dc] in next dtr. ch 4. Skip ch-2 space. [dc, ch 4, dtr, ch 6, dtr, ch 4, dc] in ch-8 loop. ch 4.** Skip ch-2 space, and dc in next dtr. Repeat from * 4 more times, and from * to ** once. Join with sl st in initial ch 1. (See Steps 1–3.)

Rnd 3: sl st in ch-3 space, and ch 1 (counts as dc). dc in same ch-3 space. *3 dc in next ch-4 space. ch 8, and sl st in 6th ch from hook to form picot. ch 2. Skip dc, and skip ch-4 space. dc in next dtr. ch 7, and sl st in 6th ch from hook to form picot. ch 1. dtr in next ch-6 space. ch 9, and sl st in 8th ch from hook to form picot. ch 9, and sl st in 4th ch from hook to form picot. ch 4, and sl st in 1st ch of last ch 9. ch 8, and sl st in 8th ch from hook to form picot. ch 1. dtr in same ch-6 space as last dtr. ch 7, and sl st in 6th ch from hook to form picot. ch 1. dc in next dtr. ch 8, and sl st in 6th ch from hook to form picot. ch 2. Skip ch-4 space, and 3 dc in next ch-4 space.** 2 dc in the following ch-3 space. Repeat from * 4 more times, and from * to ** once. Join with sl st in initial ch 1. Fasten off; weave in ends. (See Steps 4–8.)

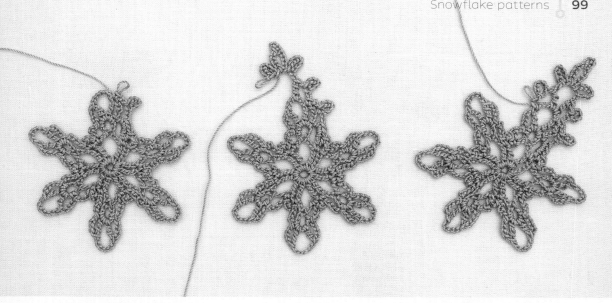

4 *3 dc in next ch-4 space. ch 8, and sl st in the sixth ch from hook to form picot. ch 2. Skip dc, and skip ch-4 space. dc in next dtr.

5 ch 7, and sl st in the sixth ch from hook to form picot. ch I. dtr in next ch-6 space. ch 9, and sl st in the eighth ch from hook to form picot. ch 9, and sl st st in the fourth ch from hook to form picot. ch 4, and sl st in the first ch of last ch 9. ch 8, and sl st in the eighth ch from hook to form picot.

6 ch I. dtr in same ch-6 space as last dtr. ch 7, and sl st in the sixth ch from hook to form picot. ch I. dc in next dtr.

7 ch 8, and sl st in the sixth ch from hook to form picot. ch 2. Skip ch-4 space, and 3 dc in next ch-4 space.** 2 dc in the following ch-3 space.

8 Repeat Steps 4–7 four more times. Begin a fifth repeat, but stop when you get to the ** in Step 7. sl st in the ch I that began the round. Fasten off and weave in ends.

Projects

Crochet snowflakes can be hung as ornaments, used to embellish clothing and homewares, or joined together to create gorgeous lace accessories. The project ideas in this section provide just a few examples.

Lavender sachets

Use crochet snowflakes to embellish lavender sachets for a beautiful and sweet-smelling addition to your home's decor.

Snowflakes used: Bariloche (pages 26–27) • Sokcho (pages 34–35) • Uppsala (pages 68–69)

Coasters

Combine several snowflakes to create gorgeous lace coasters and doilies. You can either sew your finished snowflakes together, or join them as you crochet them, by slip stitching the points of each snowflake to those of its neighbours.

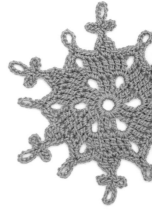

Snowflakes used: St Petersburg (pages 38–39) • Harbin (pages 60–61) • El Serrat (pages 64–65)

Child's dress

Create a winter fashion
statement by appliquéing
a sprinkle of snowflakes
to a little girl's special dress.

Snowflakes used: Bariloche (pages 26–27) • St Paul (pages 28–29) • Harbin (pages 60–61)

Garlands

Hang an elegant snowflake garland to decorate for
a holiday or event, or just to brighten up the short winter days.

Method

Crochet, block and stiffen your
snowflakes; then crochet a long
chain, attaching snowflakes as
you go with a stitch into the point.
For extra sparkle, embellish the
snowflakes with glass seed beads.
The beads can either be sewn on
the completed snowflakes, or
crocheted in place by following
these instructions:

 1 Decide how many beads
you will attach, and where
they should be placed (each
bead should fall between
two stitches).

 2 String all of the beads
on to the thread before
beginning.

 3 Start the snowflake,
allowing the beads to slide
along the thread ahead of
the stitches.

 4 When you come to a point
where you will place a bead,
slide the bead up next to the
last stitch.

 5 Use the next stitch to secure
it in place, then continue
with the pattern.

Snowflakes used: Aspen (pages 66–67) • Dingboche (pages 70–71) • St John's (pages 74–75) • Irkutsk (pages 76–77)
• Caribou (pages 84–85)

Hair bands

Celebrate wintertime with lovely seasonal hair accessories.
Attach snowflakes to a pre-made hair band, or crochet your
own bands using the instructions below.

Method

Small, compact snowflakes work
particularly well for this project.
You will want enough to lay out
a strip of overlapping snowflakes
roughly 23cm (9in) long.

 1 Block and stiffen the
snowflakes with strong
starch or fabric stiffener.

 2 Then crochet a long chain,
double the desired length
of the hair band (if the
finished band will have
a circumference of 56cm
[22in], the chain should
be 112cm (44in] long).

 3 Fold the chain in half, so
that the band is created
from a double thickness
of chain, and thread the
doubled chain through
the snowflakes.

 4 Pass one of the loose ends
of the chain through its
folded end, and join it to the
other loose end, to connect
the ends of the band.

 5 Finally, use a few stitches to
sew each snowflake to one
next to it.

Snowflakes used: Tallinn (pages 32–33) • Innsbruck (pages 56–57) • Nome (pages 58–59)

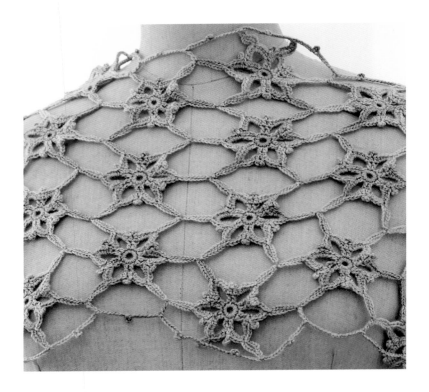

Scarf

Who says snowflakes have to be cold? Embrace the winter
weather with a cosy and memorable snowflake scarf.

Method

Choose a simple snowflake pattern
and your favourite yarn. For a
light, lacy scarf, use a lace-weight
yarn like the soft wool blend
shown here. For a heavier one,
use a thicker yarn and a more
solid snowflake pattern.

 1 As you make each
snowflake, join it to the
neighbouring snowflakes by
slip stitching at the points.

 **2** If you like, use chains and
picots to create a simple
edging for the finished scarf
(this is particularly helpful if
the snowflakes have long
points that need support).

 3 Soak the scarf in cold water,
block it on towels and wear
it all winter long.

Snowflakes used: Winnipeg (page 36–37)

Symbols and abbreviatons

Below you will find information on the abbreviations, symbols and terminology used in the Snowflake patterns chapter (see pages 18–99) and elsewhere in this book.

English/American terminology

The patterns in this book use English terminology, which differs somewhat from American terminology. You may find this list of English terms and their American equivalents useful.

English	American
double crochet (**dc**)	single crochet (**sc**)
half treble (**htr**)	half double crochet (**hdc**)
treble (**tr**)	double crochet (**dc**)
double treble (**dtr**)	treble (**tr**)
triple treble (**trtr**)	double treble (**dtr**)

Pattern notes

■ **Asterisks (* **)**
Indicate material to be repeated, with starting and ending points:

■ **Repeat from ***
Repeat all instructions that you have been given, starting with the last *.

■ **Repeat from * to ****
Repeat the instructions between the last * and the ** that follows it.

In snowflakes, it is common for a group of stitches to be repeated several times, and then partially repeated again:

■ **Repeat from * 4 times, and from * to ** once more**
Repeat all instructions, starting at the last *, 4 times. Then begin a fifth repetition, but stop when you get to the **.

Basic symbols and abbreviations

◦	Chain		ch	Chain
●	Slip stitch		sl st	Slip stitch
+	Double crochet		dc	Double crochet
⊤	Half treble crochet		htr	Half treble crochet
⊤	Treble crochet		tr	Treble crochet
⊤	Double treble crcochet		dtr	Double treble crcochet

Index

Index

Credits

Publisher acknowledgements:
All step-by-step and other images
are the copyright of Quarto
Publishing plc. While every effort
has been made to credit
contributors, Quarto would like
to apologise should there be any
omissions or errors – and would be
pleased to make the appropriate
correction for future editions of
the book.

Author acknowledgements:
I'd like to thank my family for
their support and patience, and
everyone at Quarto for their help
and encouragement.

With special thanks to Coats &
Clark for supplying the Aunt
Lydia's thread used in this book.

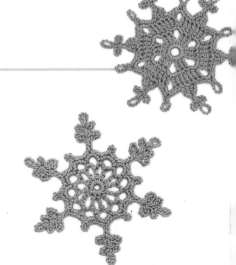